The Seven Deadly Sins

and

Spiritual Transformation

John T. Mabray

PRESS

Buck,

May the Lord bless and keep you and yours, now and forever!

John

Table of Contents

Dedication

With thanksgiving for all of God's mercies to me,

I humbly dedicate this book to the congregation of

Rivermont Evangelical Presbyterian Church,

Lynchburg, Virginia;

and to the member of that congregation dearest to my heart,

Catherine,

whose patient understanding,

steadfast support, spontaneous laughter,

and unconditional love

have sustained, encouraged, and comforted me through

thirty years of marriage and

twenty-six years of ordained pastoral ministry.

Acknowledgments

When acknowledging and expressing thanks to those who have contributed to a particular endeavor, perhaps especially in ministry, it is never possible to name everyone and there is always the possibility of failing to mention someone whose name surely ought to have been on the list. Such is the case here.

God has been very good to me. His grace, mercy, steadfast love, and faithfulness have been lavished upon me through his providential care and spiritual blessings. Among those who have shown me the love and faithfulness of God are, first of all, my parents, Jack P. Mabray and the late Bettie Sue Trimble Mabray. Thanks to them, my life from infancy has been shaped by Christian faith and nurture. I would like to thank my father, also, for the particular encouragement and support he has given for the publication of this book.

I am deeply grateful to the congregations which nurtured me in the Christian faith from infancy, through adolescence, into adulthood – The Newellton Union Church of Newellton, Louisiana; Covenant Presbyterian and First Presbyterian, both of Monroe, Louisiana; and Highland Park Presbyterian Church of Dallas, Texas – and to those congregations which I have been honored and blessed to serve as pastor: The First Presbyterian Church of Warren, Arkansas; Covenant Presbyterian Church of Monroe, Louisiana; and

Rivermont Evangelical Presbyterian Church of Lynchburg, Virginia, which I presently serve as Senior Pastor.

My two Associate Pastors, Ron Cox and Chris Deneen, are a great support in ministry. Their faithful service in their respective areas of ministry enables me to focus on the ministry of the word. The Ruling Elders and Deacons join together with the pastors in leading and serving the congregation. In addition, the support staff here undergirds the ongoing life of the church, and the secretarial staff keeps things running as smoothly as possible and compensates for my many absent-minded blunders. The members of the congregation continue to be a great encouragement to me, especially as I labor in preaching and teaching. The idea for this book really came from a number of members who thought that my sermon series on "The Seven Deadly Sins" should have a broader audience. I thank them all for their partnership in the gospel.

I am especially appreciative to those members who have worked together with me in the production of this book. Eileen Lass and Curtis Eshleman served as proofreaders, painstakingly poring over revision after revision, forcing me to go back through the drafts again and again to "get it right," and offering helpful suggestions which greatly improved the manuscript. Andrew Schwartz contributed his creative talents to the visual design of the book, and Matt Bradner helped me sharpen some key ideas. Catherine, my greatest supporter, also read the manuscript with a keen eye for detail and an impeccable instinct for proper syntax!

No list of acknowledgments would be complete without a special word of thanks to my dear friend, brother in Christ, and pastoral mentor, Lowell B. Sykes (Pastor Emeritus of this congregation), who has taught me by word and example what it means to preach "Christ, and him crucified" (1 Corinthians 2:2).

Foreword

In the fourth century, a monk named John Cassian (360-435) first enumerated a list of vices which was later refined by Pope Gregory the Great (540-604) and has become known as "the seven deadly sins": *pride, envy, anger, sloth, greed, gluttony,* and *lust.*

This book addresses "the seven deadly sins" from the perspective of Reformed Christian doctrine, particularly as articulated in the **Westminster Confession of Faith and Catechisms** and the **Heidelberg Catechism**.[1] With regard to a list of sins identified as "deadly," it is important at the outset to note:

> Just as there is no sin so small that it does not deserve damnation, so there is no sin so great that it can bring damnation upon those who truly repent.[2]
> (Romans 6:23; Romans 5:12; Matthew 12:36; James 2:10; Isaiah 55:7; Romans 8:1; Isaiah 1:16, 18)

That statement of the Westminster Confession of Faith affirms not only the potentially "deadly" nature of any and every sin, but also the amazing grace of God which is sufficient for the forgiveness of all the sins of those who turn to God in repentance through faith in Jesus Christ.

The "seven deadly sins" are not deeds but rather sinful attitudes or dispositions which underlie and lead to acts of sin, whether sins of commission or omission. In this book, each of the "seven deadly sins" serves as a focal point on which we will examine ourselves – our attitudes, inclinations, behaviors, and habits – in order to discover those specific areas of our lives in which we need to exercise particular repentance for the sake of spiritual transformation.

Not all of these seven sins manifest themselves in all of us in the same way to the same degree. Throughout the various stages of our individual lives, these sinful inclinations will have varying degrees of influence and expression. But, in one way or another and to one degree or another, these sinful dispositions reside in our sinful nature; and, therefore, in one way or another and to one degree or another, we commit particular sins arising out of these sinful inclinations. We therefore need to deal with them, by way of genuine repentance, trusting in Christ, seeking his grace for the transformation of our lives.

There is no particular verse or passage of Scripture in which these seven sins – *pride, envy, anger, sloth, greed, gluttony,* and *lust* – are listed together. In that sense, this list of "the seven deadly sins" is a purely human construct. But I do think that there is good spiritual wisdom and insight in the identification of "the seven deadly sins" because the list covers every aspect of our human nature. *Pride* and *envy* are sins of the inner spirit, sinful attitudinal dispositions at the very root of the fallen human personality. *Anger* and *sloth* have to do with the soul; that is, how we relate to and respond to the external world, at the emotional and volitional (exercise of the will) levels. The last three – *greed, gluttony,* and *lust* – all have to do with our appetites, our affections and desires, as bodily creatures.

Pride and *envy* reside in the inner **spirit**; *anger* and *sloth* are expressions of the **soul** in relation to the external world;

greed, *gluttony*, and *lust* corrupt the creaturely instincts of the **body**. Thus, this list of "the seven deadly sins" covers the gamut of our fallen humanity – spirit, soul, and body – and it reminds us that Original Sin pervades the totality of our being and that there is no aspect of human nature which is not tainted and corrupted by sin. These seven are therefore "deadly" in the sense that they are sinful dispositions which, if given free rein, would take over our lives – spirit, soul, and body – and lead us further and further down the wide road of destruction (Matthew 7:13). Were it not for the persevering grace of the Holy Spirit within true believers, convicting us of sin and enabling us to repent of our sins, we would have no means of victory over the deadly power of our sins.

The reader will note the use of the Westminster Confession of Faith and Catechisms and the Heidelberg Catechism throughout the book. This reflects the theological tradition out of which I write. I have been a Presbyterian all of my life, and an ordained Presbyterian Minister for twenty-six years. Of course, there are resources from other Christian traditions which aid us in living the Christian life, but these are the ones which have been most significant and helpful to me. Let it be understood, however, that this book is written with the conviction that the Bible is the word of God written, uniquely and fully inspired by the Holy Spirit, the rule of faith and life, and the supreme and final authority on all matters on which it speaks. The confessions and catechisms of the Reformed faith seek only to teach in a systematic manner what the Bible itself reveals.

Finally, I would appeal to the reader to read this book not merely for information but primarily for *transformation*. My prayer is that whatever is in accord with the word of God would be blessed by his Spirit to help you, and that whatever may be in error would be quickly and completely forgotten by you or corrected by a more able teacher.

To God be the glory!

Introduction

Spiritual Transformation

What is sanctification?
Sanctification is the work of God's free grace
by which our whole person is made new in the
image of God, and we are made more and more able
to become dead to sin and alive to righteousness.
(2 Thessalonians 2:13; Ephesians 4:23-24; Romans 6:4-6, 14;
Romans 8:1-4)

THE SHORTER CATECHISM in Modern English, #35[1]

I appeal to you therefore, brothers, by the mercies of God, to present your bodies as a living sacrifice, holy and acceptable to God, which is your spiritual worship. Do not be conformed to this world, but be transformed by the renewal of your mind, that by testing you may discern what is the will of God, what is good and acceptable and perfect (Romans 12:1-2).

Is your life different, and *becoming different*, because God the Father through the Lord Jesus Christ by the power of the Holy Spirit is at work in you?

That's a question that I have to ask *myself* about *myself.* Is my life any different, is my life becoming any different, because the Spirit of God is at work in me, changing me?

Do you want to change? Do you want to *be changed*? Or are you comfortable with yourself just as you are? Satisfied with yourself, just as you are?

There are other questions, though, that might lurk underneath or overshadow these questions, such as: Do I really believe that I *can* be changed? Or have I given up, in despair and resignation, as though any hope for real change and growth in my spiritual life were futile?

This is a book about spiritual transformation. The foundational verse is Romans 12:2a, "Do not be conformed to this world, but be transformed by the renewal of your mind ... ."

As Christians – believers in Christ, in union with him through faith in him by the grace of God the Father and the power of the Holy Spirit – we are called to *be transformed*; in fact, we are commanded to be transformed. That, in itself, is an interesting and important concept: We are commanded to *be transformed*; that is, we are commanded, in this case, not to do something, but rather to let something be done to us. We are commanded to be *passively active*, or *actively passive*. It is not something that we can do for ourselves by ourselves; but it is a work of grace in which we actively participate, by allowing God to transform us through the renewal of our minds by his written word (the Bible) and the work of his Holy Spirit. And, as believers in Christ, we are promised transformation: personal spiritual transformation into the likeness of Jesus Christ, with real, practical, visible effect in our lives – inner transformation which makes a real difference in our daily lives. That is God's promise and that is our calling. The Scriptures say it in various ways; for example,

> ... *work out your own salvation* with fear and trembling, *for it is God who works in you*, both to will and to work for his good pleasure (Philippians 2:12b-13, emphasis mine);

and,

> ...may the God of peace who brought again from the dead our Lord Jesus, the great shepherd of the sheep, by the blood of the eternal covenant, *equip you with everything good that you may do his will, working in us that which is pleasing in his sight*, through Jesus Christ, to whom be glory forever and ever (Hebrews 13:20, emphasis mine).

In Christian spiritual growth and transformation (sanctification), we can work *only* because God works in us. Our work in the spiritual life is made possible only by God's work of grace in us, and our work is our response to God's work of grace in us. Therefore, we need to understand some very important points. This is not a book on "self-improvement." The Bible doesn't teach anything about "self-improvement" in the spiritual life through our own human efforts. This is not a "self-help" book. The gospel of Jesus Christ is for those who are painfully aware that with regard to their relationship with God they are desperately *self-helpless* and without hope in and of themselves. Yes: *With regard to our relationship with God, we are desperately self-helpless and without hope in and of ourselves.* This book, then, is not about "human potential" in terms of spiritual transformation by merely human techniques or human efforts at moral improvement. Whatever else we might say about "human potential" deriving from the fact that we are created in the image and likeness of God, we must never underestimate the fact that we are fallen creatures corrupted by the reality of sin, and that in our deceitful hearts there is the potential for all manner of evil.

That might not sound like "positive thinking," and it might not sound very "uplifting" right here at the start; but for those who, by the grace of the Spirit of God, have ears to hear, the gospel of Jesus Christ and the promise of personal transformation through him by the power of the Holy Spirit is the most hope-filled, uplifting message because it's true and real and effective, and because it straightforwardly faces and powerfully deals with the real issue which troubles our lives. The real issue which troubles our lives is sin. And what we want – the change we want and the transformation we need in order to live happier and more fulfilled lives – is deliverance from sin: cleansing from the guilt of sin and freedom from the power of sin. That cleansing and that freedom come from Jesus Christ. They are his gifts to us: the gift of our justification, our right standing with God, our peace with God; and the gift of our sanctification, which is another word for the transformation of our lives by the working of the Holy Spirit in us, so that we, by God's grace, are changed more nearly into the likeness of Jesus Christ, restored to the true humanity we were intended to be, for the glory of God.

Let me make sure that we really understand – and do not misunderstand – the starting point of this book. This book is not about "how to become good enough for God." This book is not about how to "get our act together" enough so that God will accept us or approve of us. We all fell from that standard a long time ago, and we can't pull ourselves up by our own bootstraps to put ourselves in a good position with God. That's the bad news. But the good news – the gospel of Jesus Christ – is that *that* righteous requirement, that requirement to be "good enough," has already been fulfilled for us. That perfect standard has already been met for us, on our behalf. Jesus Christ is our righteousness.

> For our sake he [God the Father] made him [Jesus Christ] to be sin who knew no sin, so that in him [in Jesus Christ] we might become the righteousness of God (2 Corinthians 5:21, insertions mine).

If you are searching, trying to find a way to be "good enough" for God, trying to find a way to earn God's favor, struggling and trying harder: The answer is not in your works or efforts or self-improvement. The answer is in Jesus Christ and his work for you. I appeal to you, by the mercies of God, to receive that righteousness which Christ has already worked for you and offers to you as a free gift. When you come to him in faith, he receives you, and you receive his righteousness. That's the gospel! In Christ alone, in union with him through faith in him alone, we have our right standing with the Father. He is the One who met all the righteous requirements of God for us, and in his sinless perfection he offered himself up as the substitutionary sacrifice for all our sins!

If you are burdened with guilt because of something you've done in your past, and you wish there were something you could do to undo that, to make it right or wipe it away as if it had never happened, so that it no longer stood as an obstacle between you and God, but you know you can't do that – the good news is that there is Someone who can! Jesus Christ, "the righteous," bore your sins "in his body on the tree" to cleanse you, to wipe out every blot, to set you free from the guilt of your sins! (1 John 2:1; 1 Peter 2:24)

That's the gospel, the good news, upon which this entire book is founded and upon which all true spiritual transformation is founded. We need to believe that gospel as we move forward.

This transformed life in Christ is lived only in response to God's mercy through Jesus Christ. That's how Romans 12 begins:

"I appeal to you, therefore, brothers, by the *mercies of God* ... ."

Mark that. The "mercies of God" are the foundation and the motivation of the transformed life. The "mercies of God" are the mercies revealed in Jesus Christ, who was "delivered up for our trespasses and raised for our justification" (Romans 4:25). The "mercies of God" are the mercies through Christ by which we have the victory over sin and death (1 Corinthians 15:56-57). The "mercies of God" are the mercies through Christ by which we are assured that "for those who love God, all things work together for good," and, therefore, that there is nothing in all creation which "will be able to separate us from the love of God in Christ Jesus our Lord" (Romans 8:28, 39).

This is not about trying to be good enough for God. It's about responding to God's mercies and opening yourself up to be transformed "by the renewal of your mind" (Romans12:2).

But what is the renewal of your mind? The renewal of your mind is the spiritual illumination of your mind which enables you to understand spiritual truths revealed in Scripture, further enabling you to understand yourself and the world in a way consistent with God's revealed truth. This is not some secret, special ability granted only to a few super-spiritual people. It is the work of the Holy Spirit promised to all believers in Christ. Chief among these spiritual truths revealed in Scripture is the reality of our sinfulness and, therefore, our need for repentance. One of the primary ways that God renews our minds is that he enables us to see our sins as he sees them, so that we will hate them and turn away from them and seek his mercy for the transformation of our lives.

J. C. Ryle, in the nineteenth century, wrote:

He that wishes to attain right views about Christian holiness must begin by examining the vast and solemn subject of sin. He must dig down very low if he would build high. ...The plain truth is that a right knowledge of sin lies at the root of all saving Christianity.[2]

More recently, near the end of the twentieth century, Cornelius Plantinga wrote:

...I am trying to retrieve an old awareness that has slipped and changed in recent decades. The awareness of sin used to be our shadow. Christians hated sin, feared it, fled from it, grieved over it. ...But the shadow has dimmed. Nowadays, the accusation *you have sinned* is often said with a grin, and with a tone that signals an inside joke. ... To put it mildly, modern consciousness does not encourage moral reproach; in particular, it does not encourage self-reproach.[3]

This book is a call to self-examination, to see the sin within us; and therefore it is a call to self-reproach, so that in response to God's mercies, we will cry out to God in repentance and seek, by his grace and power, to be transformed by the renewal of our minds. That's the big idea and the goal of this book. Why? Because real spiritual transformation takes place only when we are willing to repent of our personal and particular sins.[4] And this repentance from sin has to do not only with initial conversion (when we first believed in Christ), but with the ongoing, lifelong process of *continual* repentance as we continue to trust in Christ for our salvation.

Why is continual repentance, a lifelong turning from sin, important? Well, let me ask you: How often do you take out the trash? Once a day? Twice a week? Well, I hope the answer to that question is: "As often as necessary." Because if you don't take out the trash as often as necessary, you end up living in a pile of garbage. And it stinks. Repentance is an ongoing, transformative process.

In the chapters which follow, we're going to take a look at the reality of sin in us. We're going to consider the ways in which our sinful nature and our actual sins deform us and defile us and destroy our relationships and deface the image of God in us. We're going to consider the ways in which sin works as a corrupting power, polluting and perverting that which is good and true and beautiful. And we are going to look particularly at the sins (or sinful dispositions) enumerated historically, since the fourth century, as the "seven deadly sins": *pride, envy, anger, sloth, greed, gluttony,* and *lust.*

Now, in addition to these seven specific sins, *every* sin, *any* sin beyond these seven, is potentially a "deadly" sin. Every sin deserves God's wrath and curse, though some sins are more heinous, more evil, than others.[5] But, at the same time,

> Just as there is no sin so small that it does not deserve damnation, so there is no sin so great that it can bring damnation upon those who truly repent.[6]

Let me repeat that final phrase: *"There is no sin so great that it can bring damnation upon those who truly repent."* So, when I refer to the "seven deadly sins" and you see them in your life (as I see them in mine), do not despair as if there were no cure, no remedy. We have a great cure, a great remedy: Jesus Christ, the sinless Savior who is the Victor over sin and death. He is able and willing to deliver you from all your sins – not only to cleanse you from the guilt of sin, but also to free you, to set you free, from the power of sin.

And that – *that!* — is what this study is all about. It's not about "sin," not ultimately. It's not about the "seven deadly sins," not really. This book is really about the Savior from sin: Jesus Christ the righteous, who was "delivered up [crucified] for our trespasses and raised for our justification" (Romans 4:25, insertion mine). This book is about Jesus Christ our Savior who, through the power of the Holy Spirit, transforms our lives, remakes us, renovates us, so that we become less and less conformed to this world, less and less dominated and controlled by our sinful nature, and more and more transformed into Christlikeness, so that we are more and more enabled and empowered by the Holy Spirit to live lives full of joy, pleasing to God, and fruitful for his kingdom, all for his glory.

"Do not be conformed to this world, but be transformed by the renewal of your mind ..." (Romans 12:2a). That is an ongoing, lifelong process. Jesus said, "If anyone would come after me, let him deny himself, take up his cross daily, and follow me" (Luke 9:23). The transformation of our lives involves dying daily – dying to self and living for Christ. The Scripture says that "he himself bore our sins in his body on the tree, that we might die to sin and live to righteousness" (1 Peter 2:24). There it is: dying and living. The Scripture exhorts us to "cast off the works of darkness and put on the armor of light" (Romans 13:12) – casting off, putting on – and to "put off your old self ... and put on the new self" (Ephesians 4:24); and to "put on" or to "clothe" ourselves with "compassion, kindness, humility, meekness, and patience ..." (Colossians 3:12).

This is the rhythm of repentance and renewal: dying and living; putting off and putting on; repenting and being renewed; turning away from the world, and turning toward Jesus Christ, being continually transformed into his likeness. All of it is by God's work within us, by the power of the Holy Spirit through the grace of our Lord Jesus Christ.

Do we participate in this work? *Yes, by the power he provides!* Is there hope that we will really grow in the grace of our Lord Jesus Christ, so that our lives will be transformed for his glory? *Yes, through the promise of the gospel!* Is this something that you long for in the depths of your soul? Are you willing to cry out to God for the personal transformation of your life? Are you willing to examine yourself? Are you willing to see your sins as God sees them, and confess them, plead for forgiveness, and seek the transforming power of the Holy Spirit in your life? Are you willing to die daily, to put off the old man, to put on the new, and to be renewed in the likeness of Christ, and to pursue "the holiness without which no one will see the Lord" (Hebrews 12:14)? May the Lord, in his mercy and by his grace, make us willing, and place that desire within us, to be not conformed to this world, but *transformed* for the glory of his name!

For Further Meditation and Spiritual Exercise

A CALL TO CONFESSION

What shall we say then? Are we to continue in sin that grace may abound? By no means! How can we who died to sin still live in it? Do you not know that all of us who have been baptized into Christ Jesus were baptized into his death? We were buried therefore with him by baptism into death, in order that, just as Christ was raised from the dead by the glory of the Father, we too might walk in newness of life (Romans 6:1-4).

A PRAYER OF CONFESSION

Father of all mercy, I humbly confess that I have sinned against you and am unworthy to be called your child. I have yielded to the sinful inclinations of my deceitful heart and, in word and deed, have disobeyed your holy commands. Forgive me, O Lord, and renew the power of the Holy Spirit in me, that I may put off all the deeds of the flesh and the works of darkness. Forgive and set me free from the sins of pride, envy, anger, sloth, greed, gluttony and lust. Rid me of all bitterness, slander, malice, sexual impurity and materialistic idolatry. By your grace, produce in my life the fruit of the Spirit, that I may walk in newness of life as a person of love, joy, peace, patience, kindness, goodness, faithfulness, gentleness and self-control. Do this, I earnestly pray, for the glory of your holy name, by the power of your Holy Spirit, through your holy Son, Jesus Christ, in whom alone I trust for my salvation. Amen.

THE ASSURANCE OF THE GOSPEL

There is therefore now no condemnation for those who are in Christ Jesus. For the law of the Spirit of life has set you free in Christ Jesus from the law of sin and death (Romans 8:1-2).

Chapter 1

The Sin of Pride,
and the Humble Savior

Now the serpent was more crafty than any other beast
of the field that the LORD God had made. He said to
the woman, "Did God actually say, 'You shall not
eat of any tree in the garden'?" And the woman said
to the serpent, "We may eat of the fruit of the trees
in the garden, but God said, 'You shall not eat of the
fruit of the tree that is in the midst of the garden,

neither shall you touch it, lest you die.'" But the serpent said to the woman, "You will not surely die. For God knows that when you eat of it your eyes will be opened, and you will be like God, knowing good and evil." So when the woman saw that the tree was good for food, and that it was a delight to the eyes, and that the tree was to be desired to make one wise, she took of its fruit and ate, and she also gave some to her husband who was with her, and he ate. Then the eyes of both were opened, and they knew that they were naked. And they sewed fig leaves together and made themselves loincloths. And they heard the sound of the LORD God walking in the garden in the cool of the day, and the man and his wife hid themselves from the presence of the LORD God among the trees of the garden. But the LORD God called to the man and said to him, "Where are you?" And he said, "I heard the sound of you in the garden, and I was afraid, because I was naked, and I hid myself." He said, "Who told you that you were naked? Have you eaten of the tree of which I commanded you not to eat?" The man said, "The woman whom you gave to be with me, she gave me fruit of the tree, and I ate." Then the LORD God said to the woman, "What is this that you have done?" The woman said, "The serpent deceived me, and I ate" (Genesis 3:1-13).

Throughout this book, words and phrases such as *spiritual transformation, growing in grace, growing in Christlikeness,* and *sanctification* mean basically the same thing, referring to the work of the Holy Spirit to transform our lives "from the inside out" so that our lives more fully and truly express the reality of Christ's life in us. In the gospel of Jesus Christ, we hear not only the promise of forgiveness but also the call to spiritual transformation. "Do not be conformed to this world [to its sinful attitudes and behaviors], but be transformed by the renewal of your mind" (Romans 12:2a, insertion mine).

Renewal of our mind takes place, first of all, as the Holy Spirit, through the word of God in Scripture, reveals our sins to us and enables us to see our sins as God sees them – as heinous and hateful – so that we hate our sins and mourn over them and flee from them, and then turn to Jesus Christ for (1) the *forgiveness of* our sins and (2) the *freedom from* our sins. This fleeing from our sins and turning to Jesus Christ is what the Bible means by *repentance* (see the Shorter Catechism #87, above).

This renewal through repentance is a *continual* process in the life of the believer, and we are called and commanded to participate in and with the work of the Holy Spirit in the transformation of our lives. There will be no true transformation of our lives without continual repentance from our personal sins and a sincere endeavor to follow Christ in newness of life every day.

But remember: Christian spiritual transformation is not a matter of "self-improvement." It is a matter of spiritual renovation. Christian spiritual transformation is not a matter of "self-help." We are helpless to help ourselves, and our only help is in Jesus Christ by the power of the Holy Spirit. And true Christian spiritual transformation is not about "trying hard" to be "good enough" for God. We can never meet that standard; but there is One who has met that righteous standard perfectly, "Jesus Christ the righteous" (1 John 2:1). **Jesus Christ is our righteousness; he is our "good enough-ness" before God.** As our righteous substitute, he suffered for our sins and paid the penalty in full, dying for us in our place. As our risen Savior, victorious over death, he clothes us in his perfect righteousness. In union with Jesus Christ through faith in him, we stand forgiven and clothed in his righteousness before God the Father, accepted and beloved.

Therefore, spiritual transformation has nothing to do with trying to improve ourselves, help ourselves, or be "good enough" for God; rather, it is all about responding to the mercies of God and seeking to live for his glory, motivated by gratitude for his goodness and grace.

That was a long review of the introductory points, but we must be clear in our minds and assured in our hearts that the spiritual transformation of our lives is a work of God's grace: God's work of grace *for* us on the cross, and God's work of grace *in* us by the power of the Holy Spirit.

This process of personal transformation into Christlikeness is never perfected in this life. This is a very important spiritual principle that we must understand. As a Christian grows in grace, as a believer is transformed more and more into Christlikeness, his or her need for Christ's grace and mercy never diminishes! To put it another way: More Christlikeness in our lives does *not* mean less need of Christ in our lives!

Here's an illustration: The process of spiritual transformation (sanctification) is *not* like learning to ride a bicycle. What do I mean? Well, to learn to ride a bicycle, you probably started with a tricycle. Then came the bike with the training wheels. Then the training wheels came off, and your mother or father, or an older sibling or someone else, stood beside you and propped you up and balanced you and ran alongside you to catch you when you teetered one way or the other. Then, in one of those magic moments, it happened: You were riding *all on your own*! You didn't need training wheels, and you didn't need anybody running along beside you. You could ride, and you would always be able to ride your bike, all by yourself!

That's *not* what happens in spiritual growth and transformation. We *never* become self-sufficient. We *never* become independent. We *never* grow to the point of no need. Growing in grace does *not* result in needing Christ less! Growing into his likeness does *not* result in needing less of his grace and mercy and power! It's just the opposite! As a believer grows in grace, he or she becomes increasingly aware of his or her desperate need for Christ in all his saving power! So, here's the point: **There is no true holiness without true humility**.

If you are growing in grace and holiness, you will *not* say, "I do not need as much grace and mercy as I once did." To the contrary, if you are truly growing in grace and holiness into the likeness of Christ, if you are making real progress in the faith, you will become increasingly aware of your indwelling sin, increasingly aware of the great discrepancy between your sinfulness and God's holiness, increasingly aware of your desperate need for God's free and undeserved mercy upon your life, and *increasingly amazed* at the wonders of the riches of the mercies of God toward you! In this life, the horizon of sanctification is always ever-expanding and moving forward ahead of us. The farther we go in the journey of grace through this life following Jesus, the more we will realize *how much farther* we have to go. If we are growing in grace, we will have an increasing sense of our total dependence upon Christ, *not* an increasing *independence* from Christ.

And that gets us to the first of the "seven deadly sins," because the first of the "seven deadly sins" is the sin which desires and declares **independence** from God: the sin of **pride**. *Pride*: "the mother" of all sins. *Pride*: the primordial sin of Adam and Eve in the Garden of Eden.

But before we go further about the sin of pride, let's take a moment to define our terms. The word "pride" has differing connotations, different nuances, different uses in differing contexts. Not all "pride" is sinful pride. For example, when we as parents see our children attain a new level of skill or ability (such as riding a bike by themselves!), or see our children achieve a worthy goal, or see them mature as young

Christian men or women, we are rightly "proud" of them and "proud" for them in the sense that we rejoice in their success, we rejoice in God's blessings upon them. There is nothing sinful about that.

In fact, in the New Testament there are a few different words which can be translated into English as "pride." Some of those Greek words clearly have the more negative connotation of "arrogance," but others have the more positive connotation of "rejoicing over" or "celebrating" good success. So, for example, the Apostle Paul could write to the Romans,

> In Christ Jesus ...I have reason to be *proud* of my work for God. For I will not venture to speak of anything except what Christ has accomplished through me... (Romans 15:17, emphasis mine).

To the Corinthians, because of their faith, Paul wrote, "I have great *pride* in you" (2 Corinthians 7:40, emphasis mine); and he encouraged the Philippians to persevere in faithfulness so that "I may be *proud* that I did not run in vain or labor in vain" (Philippians 2:16, emphasis mine).

We understand, then, that there is a kind of "pride" which is not sinful pride. But the pride which concerns us here in this chapter is that pride which prompts us to seek independence from God. What is the difference between appropriate pride and *sinful* pride? Sinful pride is the desire to steal God's glory for ourselves, to put ourselves in the place of God, claiming his glory as our own. That is basically what Adam and Eve sought to do by eating the forbidden fruit.

We were created for glory. Humanity was created "in the image of God" to reflect the glory of God on the earth (Genesis 1:27). But that glory for which we were created and with which we were endowed by God was intended to serve as a mirror image of his glory, so that his glory would fill the

32

earth through us. Sinful pride, however, seeks to dethrone God and claim his glory for ourselves. Sinful pride stirs within us not only the desire to be independent from God, but also the desire to *be* God: to think and act and live as though I *were* God.

"You will not surely die. For God knows that when you eat of it your eyes will be opened, and you will be like God, knowing good and evil" (Genesis 3:5).

"You will not surely die; oh no, you just won't be dependent upon God anymore. You'll be as wise as he is, and you'll be free to make your own decisions. You won't need him to tell you what to do ...or not to do."

So when the woman saw that the tree was good for food [*that makes sense, so why not?*], and that it was a delight to the eyes [*and why shouldn't she enjoy it?*], and that the tree was desired to make one wise [*and with wisdom comes power*], she took some of its fruit and ate, and she also gave some to her husband who was with her and he ate (Genesis 3:6, insertions mine).

And by that disobedience, by that desire to be independent from God, by that desire to *be* God, the whole human race was bound in the shackles of slavery to sin. And the lock on those shackles is the sin of pride: **the desire to be God and to grasp his glory as our own.**

It's very deep-seated in us, so deeply seated that we sometimes can't even see it. It comes out in various ways. Most obviously, it comes out in the arrogance and the haughtiness of the strong, the presumptuously self-sufficient, the rich and powerful in this world who believe that they have no need of God.[1] This is the pride which is most often condemned in the

Scriptures of the Old and New Testaments. This is the pride which manifests itself in bold wickedness, in blatant disobedience to God's law, without the fear of God.

> In the pride of his face, the wicked does not seek him;
> all his thoughts are, "There is no God" (Psalm 10:4).

Now you might say, *"But that doesn't sound like me. I don't have that kind of pride."* OK, you and I might not act like Nebuchadnezzar or Herod the Great or some arrogant Hollywood celebrity or presumptuous politician; but what about my willfulness to have things my way? What about my resistance to and defiance of God's law in my own personal life? Every sin is an act of pride because every sin is an act which attempts to deny God his sovereign rights or to dethrone God from his sovereign throne. Every sin is an attempt to declare our independence from God, which, in practical reality, is the same thing as saying, "In the pride of his face, the wicked does not seek him; all his thoughts are, 'There is no God'" (Psalm 10:4).

And what about the pride of superiority, or supposed superiority, or wished-for superiority over others? Why do we say those cutting little things about others? Why do we try to bring someone else down? So that we can appear superior! Well, what is this desire for superiority? Is it not grasping to be God?

And why is it that I am so concerned about how I appear to others, how well I am thought of by others, how I compare to others? *Am I as handsome as he is? Am I as smart as she is? Am I as financially prosperous as he is? Am I as popular as she is? Am I as powerful as he is? Am I as talented as she is?* What's all that about? It's about being revered as a god or goddess, and being happy if we are, and mad or sad if we're not. It's about pride. It's about measuring ourselves against others and trying to find a comfort zone of self-sufficiency and self-justification – independent of God's judgment, and independent of God's grace – which is the same thing as putting ourselves in the place of God. Why do we judge others and judge ourselves according to some standard we have made up in our minds? Aren't we just grasping to be God?

Pride manifests itself in ways other than the arrogance or self-sufficiency of the rich, strong, powerful, and beautiful. Self-pity is really just the other side of the same coin. One person gets attention and exercises power and control by being haughty and flashy and domineering; another person gets attention and exercises power and control by being pitiful and victimized and manipulative. It's still pride; it's still rebellion against God; it's still grasping to be God.

Pride is that deep-seated craving for *self-glory*: that deep-seated self-centeredness which perceives the world to be revolving around *me* or demands that the world revolve around *me* and which rebels in anger or miserable self-pity when the world doesn't revolve around *me*.

Here's a simple illustration. Take a look at the word *pride*, letter by letter:

P-R-I-D-E.

What's right in the center of "pride"? The letter **I.**

I am right in the center of pride!

How fitting it is that, in the providence of God, he gave us, in the English language, a perfect lesson in the nature of pride simply by the way we spell it! *I* am also in the center of *sin*!

So, what are you going to do with your sinful pride? There's only one thing for me to do with mine. Crucify it. Crucify it, every day. I have to catch myself … catch my *self* … catch my *self* in its sinful resistance to God's word, catch my *self* in its craving for self-centered attention, catch my *self* in its despairing self-pity, catch my *self* in its grasping for glory, catch my *self* in its declaration of independence from God, and crucify it.

What might that look like in your life? I don't know exactly what it will look like for you. Ask the Lord to show you. You'll know it when you see it. But a few possible examples:

It might look like saying, "I was wrong, and I was in the wrong. That was a sinful thing to say (or do). I'm sorry. Please forgive me." And don't say, "but ... ."

It might look like saying, "I forgive you, and I won't hold this against you."

It might mean catching your *self* right before you say that humorous but unkind word about someone else, and crucifying your desire to appear superior.

It might mean not taking offense when someone says something mean or rude or careless to you or about you: not paying too much attention to it, not stewing over it, not resenting it, not replaying it over and over again in your mind with exaggerated elaborations in imaginary conversations. Crucify the pride which too easily takes offense.

What does it mean to crucify the pride? It means turning to Jesus Christ, the *humble* Savior. Consider this: **It took the humility of Jesus Christ, the glorious Son of God, to save you and me from the sin of pride**. That's what Philippians 2:5-11 is all about:

> Have this mind among yourselves, which is yours in Christ Jesus, who, though he was in the form of God, did not count equality with God a thing to be grasped, but made himself nothing, taking the form of a servant, being born in the likeness of men. And being found in human form, he humbled himself by becoming obedient to the point of death, even death on a cross. Therefore God has highly exalted him and bestowed on

him the name that is above every name, so that at the name of Jesus every knee should bow, in heaven and on earth and under the earth, and every tongue confess that Jesus Christ is Lord, to the glory of God the Father.

Jesus Christ, the Son of God, was (and is) in very nature God. He was, and is, God the Son, the eternal Second Person of the divine Trinity. In the immeasurable, unfathomable depths of eternity past, the eternal Son of God shared equally in the power and glory of God the Father and God the Holy Spirit. But although he shared equality with God, he did not consider equality with God something to be grasped. He made himself nothing; in comparison to the eternal glory, honor, and power he enjoyed, he made himself nothing, being born in the likeness of men. And he humbled himself – he humbled himself from the position of divine glory to the position of a human slave – and became obedient unto death, even death on a cross.

It took the humility of the Son of God to save us from the sin of pride. It took the humility of the Son of God on a cross, for us, to save us from our self-glorifying pride. It took the humility of the Son of God upon a cross, in our place, to renew us in the image of our Creator and to restore us to our true purpose as human beings: to reflect the glory of God (Colossians 3:10).

Look to him, Jesus Christ, who died and rose for you! Only he, in his humility, can cleanse you of the guilt of sinful pride. And only he, in the power of his resurrection, can deliver you from the slavery of sinful pride. May his humility and his power renew our minds and transform our lives, so that we may truly sing from the heart, with joy and thanksgiving:

When I survey the wondrous cross,
on which the Prince of glory died,
my richest gain I count but loss,
and pour contempt on all my pride.[2]

For Further Meditation and Spiritual Exercise

A CALL TO CONFESSION

"God opposes the proud, but gives grace to the humble." Submit yourselves therefore to God. Resist the devil, and he will flee from you. Draw near to God, and he will draw near to you. Cleanse your hands, you sinners, and purify your hearts, you double-minded. Be wretched and mourn and weep. Let your laughter be turned to mourning and your joy to gloom. Humble yourselves before the Lord, and he will exalt you (James 4:6b-10).

A PRAYER OF CONFESSION

Holy Father, give me the grace of true repentance, that with a broken spirit and a contrite heart, I may humble myself before you and truly confess my sins:

The pride of my self-righteousness, which boasts in my external morality and religion;

The pride of my stiff neck, which will not submit to your holy word;

The pride of my brazen conscience, which will not ask for forgiveness;

The pride of my hard heart, which will not offer forgiveness;

The pride of my presumed superiority, which looks down upon others, and speaks cutting words to or about others;

The pride of my defensiveness, which will not let me admit that I am wrong;

The pride of my self-centeredness, which insists on having things my way;

The pride of my self-glory, which seeks to call attention to myself;

The pride of my self-pity, which enjoys the misery I choose for myself;

The pride of my despair, which rejects your grace and mercy and power to renew my life;

The pride of my self-idolatry, which deceives me into believing that I should sit upon your throne of sovereignty.

A PRAYER OF REPENTANCE AND TRANSFORMATION

Holy Father, I look to Jesus, the humble Savior who suffered death on a cross, for the forgiveness of all my sins of pride. I look to Jesus, the humble Savior now risen from the dead, for the power to set me free from the curse of sinful pride in my life. Merciful Father, enable me by the indwelling power of the Holy Spirit, to walk in humility before you and to live as a humble servant to others; to the praise of your glorious grace, through Jesus Christ my humble Savior and glorious Lord. Amen.

THE ASSURANCE OF THE GOSPEL

For thus says the One who is high and lifted up,
who inhabits eternity, whose name is Holy:
"I dwell in the high and holy place,
and also with him who is of a contrite and lowly spirit,
to revive the spirit of the lowly,
and to revive the heart of the contrite" (Isaiah 57:15).

For while we were still weak, at the right time Christ died for the ungodly. For one will scarcely die for a righteous person—though perhaps for a good person one would dare even to die— but God shows his love for us in that while we were still sinners, Christ died for us (Romans 5:6-8).

... though he (Christ Jesus) was in the form of God, (he) did not count equality with God a thing to be grasped, but made himself nothing, taking the form of a servant, being born in the likeness of men. And being found in human form, he humbled himself by becoming obedient to the point of death, even death on a cross (Philippians 2:8, insertions mine).

Chapter 2

The Sin of Envy,
and the Self-Giving Savior

What is sanctification?
Sanctification is the work of God's free grace
by which our whole person is made new in the
image of God, and we are made more and more able
to become dead to sin and alive to righteousness.
(2 Thessalonians 2:13; Ephesians 4:23-24; Romans 6:4-6, 14;
Romans 8:1-4)

THE SHORTER CATECHISM in Modern English, #35

Now Adam knew Eve his wife, and she conceived
and bore Cain, saying, "I have gotten a man with the
help of the LORD." And again, she bore his brother
Abel. Now Abel was a keeper of sheep, and Cain
a worker of the ground. In the course of time Cain
brought to the LORD an offering of the fruit of the
ground, and Abel also brought of the firstborn of
his flock and of their fat portions. And the LORD had
regard for Abel and his offering, but for Cain and his

offering he had no regard. So Cain was very angry, and his face fell. The LORD said to Cain, "Why are you angry, and why has your face fallen? If you do well, will you not be accepted? And if you do not do well, sin is crouching at the door. Its desire is for you, but you must rule over it." Cain spoke to Abel his brother. And when they were in the field, Cain rose up against his brother Abel and killed him. Then the LORD said to Cain, "Where is Abel your brother?" He said, "I do not know; am I my brother's keeper?" (Genesis 4:1-9)

"Be not conformed to this world, but be transformed by the renewal of your mind." That Scripture, Romans 12:2a, gives us the "big idea" of this book. This book is all about growing more nearly into the likeness of Jesus Christ. It's about being changed from the inside out, so that our heart and mind and soul (what we love, what we think, what we will[1]) become more and more aligned with, in accord with, reflective of, the life of Jesus Christ. In the words of the hymn,

> *Breathe on me, breath of God,*
> *fill me with life anew,*
> > *that I may love what thou dost love,*
> *and do what thou wouldst do.*[2]

It's what Scripture and the Shorter Catechism (based on Scripture) refer to as "sanctification," which, literally, refers to the process of being made "holy"[3] (see the quotation at the heading of this chapter). And, in this process of spiritual growth, as the catechism says, we "are made more and more able to become dead to sin and alive to righteousness."

But please do not misunderstand: When the catechism says that "...we are made more and more able to become dead to sin and alive to righteousness" that does __not__ mean that sin is becoming less and less of a problem in our lives, or that sin is becoming "easier" for us to deal with. *No.* It means that, to a greater degree, we will be empowered to deal more and more fully with the full extent of sin in our life. And there's nothing easy about that.

The Christian life, following Jesus, *being transformed into his likeness,* the pursuit of holiness, never gets any easier. Even when you are growing in Christlikeness by the power of the Holy Spirit within you, and you are making real progress in the Christian life, it never gets any "easier." Of course, *some things* may get "easier." For example, you may grow in self-control so that it's not as hard for you to control your impulsive, hot temper – praise the Lord for that! You may very well have a sense of growth and increasing victory in one area of your life. But as soon as you are controlling your temper, so that you don't blow up on the outside, you might find yourself dealing with that seething rage *on the inside*; and that's a much harder fight than controlling your temper. Or, having been convicted of your pride, you might intentionally seek to become more of a servant to others, but then become proud of your humility![4] Or, your growth in humility might become corrupted by sinful self-pity, and then you might be forced to face and to fight the sin of *envy* in your heart.

That gets us to the second "deadly sin" – the sin, or the sinful disposition, the sinful attitude, of *envy.* The word "envy" does not occur in the Scripture passage quoted above from Genesis 4 – the account of the first murder, when Cain killed his brother, Abel. Envy is not mentioned, but it was there, deep in Cain's heart. And that ought to be a warning to us. The Bible sees envy as a very deeply-rooted sinful disposition in the heart of fallen humanity. It is no accident or coincidence that the "primal sin," the first sin in the Garden of Eden, was a disobedience prompted by *pride.* The next sinful act mentioned in the Bible is the sinful act of murder, which was motivated by the sinful attitude of *envy*.

Now, just pause there and think about what the Bible reveals about fallen human nature: The firstborn man was a murderer. The first human brotherhood ended in murder. That has huge implications for our basic understanding of fallen human nature, doesn't it?

Think about it: Adam and Eve's sin was prompted by pride; Cain's murder of his brother, Abel, was motivated by envy. Pride and envy are closely connected, deeply rooted in the human heart, and devastating to the human soul and to human relationships. As Cornelius Plantinga has written:

> This is a motive that prompts people to slice up other people's reputations, to disparage their achievements, to minimize their virtues, to question their motives, to challenge their integrity …and, failing other ways of bringing them down, to kill them.[5]

How do we define envy? How is it different from covetousness? Basically, to covet is to want what someone else has; to envy is to resent the fact that the other *person* has it and you don't. You covet *things*; you envy *people*. Coveting places its desire on the *object* possessed by the other person; envying spews its poison upon the *person* who has what you don't have. Coveting expresses discontentment with what you have; envy is *displeasure at another's blessing*. Coveting does not necessarily affect the relationship with the other person; envy always poisons the relationship with the other person. Coveting is wanting what another person has; envy is wanting the other person *not* to have it: *"If I can't have it, neither should you!"*

Envy makes the bones rot (Proverbs 14:30). Envy poisons the soul. And envy is satisfied not when you get what you want, but when the other person loses whatever it is he or she has, or otherwise gets "cut down to size."

Let's consider the story of Cain and Abel and do an exploration into the sinful disposition of envy.

> ...the LORD had regard for Abel and his offering, but for Cain and his offering he had no regard (Genesis 4:4,5).

Now, notice that the Bible does not give us a lot of explanation about why the LORD had regard for Abel and his offering but not for Cain. The only thing that this passage says is that "Cain brought to the LORD an offering of the fruit of the ground, and Abel also brought of the firstborn of his flock and of their fat portions" (Genesis 4:3-4). We may rightly interpret that to mean that Abel brought the best offering that he could bring ("the firstborn of his flock and of their fat portions") whereas Cain brought only an "ordinary" offering to the LORD ("an offering of the fruit of the ground").

The Letter to the Hebrews (in the New Testament) tells us that "By faith Abel offered to God a more acceptable sacrifice than Cain ..." (Hebrews 11:4). Abel's offering of "the firstborn of the flock" was the outward expression of that true faith to which Hebrews refers. But, in his own mind, Cain may well have thought that he had offered a very worthy sacrifice. *"What was wrong with my sacrifice?"* he might have wondered. I want you to put yourself in Cain's place, and try to imagine Cain's experience (feel it as your own) as this verse lays it out for us:

> ...the LORD had regard for Abel and his offering, but for Cain and his offering he had no regard.

"Why not?! Why did the LORD look with favor upon Abel's offering and not mine? Why does Abel get all the attention, and not me? Why would the LORD bless him that way and not me?"

Now, we're right at the root of envy, and I hope that you can see how envy can take root in our own hearts. Every time I look at someone and see how the LORD has given him a blessing which he has not given me, and I want to know why, and I'm angry or resentful about the fact that he or she has a blessing that I don't have, then I'm right back there in the field with Cain plotting my brother's death. Do you see that?

And notice further what the Scripture says. "So Cain was very angry and his face fell" (Genesis 4:5). Why was Cain angry? He was angry because he was envious of Abel's favor with God. But notice how God responded to Cain. God does not offer Cain an explanation. God does not offer Cain an apology. God does not try to make Cain "feel better" in the moment. God calls Cain to deal with the sin of envy in his heart.

"Why are you angry, and why has your face fallen? If you do well, will you not be accepted? And if you do not do well, sin is crouching at the door. Its desire is for you, but you must rule over it" (Genesis 4:5-7).

That sin was the sin of envy. It was crouching at the door of Cain's heart, ready to pounce like a lion to devour him. And if Cain did not rule over that envy in his heart and cast it out, then envy would destroy him. And it did destroy him. Motivated and controlled by envy, Cain destroyed Abel; but as a result, envy destroyed Cain.

Here's the point for our application: Cain probably did not know why the LORD had accepted Abel's offering but not his. Cain knew only that the LORD had blessed Abel in that way, but had not blessed him in the same way. And Cain was angry about it because he was envious of his brother. **Likewise, we most often do not know why the LORD has blessed another person in the way that he has, but has not blessed us in the same way.** How do we respond to that? Will we, by the power of God's Spirit within us, destroy envy within us? Or will we allow envy to destroy our relationships and then to destroy us?

There's always going to be somebody else who has been blessed in some way you haven't been, or has been blessed in some way to a greater degree than you have been. There's always going to be someone more impressive than you in some way. Let's say you're a very good athlete, good enough in high school to get an athletic scholarship in college. When you get there, there's going to be someone else who's a little faster, a little stronger, and has a little more savvy on the field or the court. Or, let's say that you're very beautiful. There's always going to be somebody somewhere who in the eyes of someone else is more beautiful than you. Let's say that you've got a good job, you're working hard, and you're doing pretty well financially. That's saying a lot these days! But, there's always going to be somebody some-where, maybe a friend in your church, who doesn't seem to work quite as hard as you do, but always seems to be doing a little better financially than you. What are you going to do with that? You know, I'm around men everyday who are ...*taller than I am!* And, given the fact that "envy makes the bones rot," I had better not envy them because that will only make me shorter than I already am! (Proverbs 14:30). But it's not only men who are taller, but also men who are smarter, or more intellectually-gifted theologians, or better communica-tors, or more well-known and popular as preachers, or this or that or the other.

Let's not kid ourselves about not having to deal with envy in our hearts. The American culture thrives on envy. Television is filled with images and messages that incite you to envy. How about those "matchmaking" commercials, showing those thirty-second spots of perfectly matched soul mates? *(Right!)* Unintentionally, those commercials can stir up envy in the hearts of husbands and wives who are struggling with the very normal and natural conflicts that occur within all marriages. The American political process is driven to a large degree by envy, inciting class-warfare within a nation which is *supposedly* "united." To some degree at least, the whole "self-esteem" movement in certain educational circles actually rewards envy: *Why must every child in the contest be awarded a blue ribbon?*

And, in the life of the church, envy is one of those demonic forces that seeks to divide the Body. *"He is in a leadership position instead of me; she got to serve in that role instead of me; he got the recognition for something that I worked just as hard on; she always gets approval for her ideas."*

When we understand envy this way, we can see that envy often incites murder in the heart. We need to take envy very seriously because of the other incidents in the Scripture in which envy was a prime motivator of an evil deed. Do you know the story of Joseph and his coat of many colors? Why did Joseph's brothers come close to killing him but then stop short only because they could sell him into slavery? What was their motivation? Envy. Remember King Saul, and the young shepherd-hero David? Why did Saul turn against David and continually plot, like a madman, to take David's life? Envy. And, you might be surprised to discover that among the sins and sinful attitudes listed in the New Testament which describe the depths of the depravity of fallen man, envy has its place: "...**envy**, murder, strife, deceit, maliciousness" (Romans 1:29, emphasis mine); "sexual immorality,

48

impurity, sensuality, idolatry, sorcery ...**envy**, drunkenness, orgies, and things like these" (Galatians 5:20-21, emphasis mine).

Envy is one of those spiritual forces which wars against our souls. It must not be welcomed in our hearts; it must not be pampered, nursed, and fed with our pride, self-pity, resentment, bitterness, and ingratitude. We must see it in ourselves, confess it, repent of it, and then be about the spiritual work of crucifying it.

How do we do that? What does "crucifying envy" look like in real life? First of all, it looks like being thankful to God for every blessing he has given you. Every one of us is far more blessed than any one of us deserves. And second, it looks like learning the secret of contentment: contentment with who we are and what we have, by God's grace and under his blessing. Happiness consists not in the abundance of things, nor in passing beauty, nor in the fading glory of worldly fame. Our happiness can be found only in Jesus Christ, who is "the same yesterday and today and forever" (Hebrews 13:8). Third, crucifying envy means that we will "rejoice with those who rejoice" and "weep with those who weep" (Romans 12:15). Rejoice when something good happens to someone else! Rejoice with that person; don't envy that person. Celebrate God's blessing upon that person; don't resent it. And, "weep with those who weep." Take no delight in the fact that someone else must now struggle in the same way that you have had to (this is a reverse form of envy). Take no pleasure in the pain of someone else, who you think has had life too easy. Repent of your ugly envy when you are inwardly glad to hear that someone else has had trouble in his or her life. "Weep with those who weep."

But most of all, in all of these ways, look to Jesus Christ for the grace of forgiveness to cleanse you from the guilt of envy and to set you free from its corrupting power. We can't do this on our own. We need Jesus Christ and the power of his Spirit within us, changing us, transforming us.

So think about this: Why did the Jewish authorities hand Jesus over to Pontius Pilate to be crucified? What was their motive? The Bible says it was *envy*.

> ...Pilate said to them, "Whom do you want me to release for you: Barabbas, or Jesus who is called Christ?" For he knew that it was out of *envy* that they had delivered him up (Matthew 27:17-18, emphasis mine).

They – representing us – envied Jesus, who he was and what he had: the Son of God, in all the riches of his glory, honor, and power. Like Cain envying Abel, they envied Jesus; like Cain murdering his brother, they delivered up the Lord of glory to be crucified. And we are as guilty as they – please don't misunderstand. *Our* sins of envy nailed him to the cross. But the amazing irony of the gospel is that Jesus Christ is freely willing to give us all that he has!

He is freely willing to share all the riches of grace and glory *with us*! We need not envy him or anyone else! He is freely willing to call us his brothers and sisters and to raise us up to his status and standing with the Father. He's the *self-giving* Savior who gave himself for us so that with him and through him we might receive all things – the inestimable riches of the glories of heaven! And if you are a beloved child of the Father, a beloved brother or sister of the Lord Jesus Christ, if you have been born anew to "an inheritance which is imperishable, undefiled, and unfading"[6] ...*who on earth is there for you to envy?*

Jesus Christ is the self-giving Savior who has given himself for us and to us ... *"more than all in him I find!"*[7] *Crucified by our envy, he crucifies our envy,* and sets us free to live with joy and thanksgiving!

For Further Meditation and Spiritual Exercise

A CALL TO CONFESSION

(Jesus said) "From within, out of the heart of man, come evil thoughts, sexual immorality, theft, murder, adultery, coveting, wickedness, deceit, sensuality, envy, slander, pride, foolishness. All these evil things come from within, and they defile a person" (Mark 7:21-23).

Seek the LORD while he may be found; call upon him while he is near; let the wicked forsake his way, and the unrighteous man his thoughts; let him return to the LORD, that he may have compassion on him, and to our God, for he will abundantly pardon (Isaiah 55:6-7).

A PRAYER OF CONFESSION

O Lord, as your word says, "envy makes the bones rot," so I confess before you:

My envy of those more prosperous, more popular, more powerful;

My envy of those more beautiful, more talented, more successful;

My envy of those whose lives appear easy and without troubles;

My envy of those who have greater advantages and better opportunities;

My sin of envy, which keeps me from rejoicing in the blessings of others;

My sin of envy, which spoils my blessings with ingratitude;

My sin of envy, which sours my spirit and destroys my joy in life.

51

A PRAYER OF REPENTANCE AND TRANSFORMATION

Gracious heavenly Father, forgive me for my sins of envy. Have mercy upon me, and cleanse me from this rottenness in my bones and sourness in my spirit. Save me from the snare of discontentment, and deliver me from the pit of ingratitude. Fill my heart with your Spirit, that my life may be renewed with joy. You, O God, are good to all and kind in all your works; so may I rejoice in your goodness not only to me but also to others! And may Jesus Christ be everything to me, so that this world may be crucified to me, and I to the world; that I may find my fullness of life and satisfaction of soul in him alone, who died and rose again that I might be delivered from the power of envy; to the glory of your holy name. Amen.

THE ASSURANCE OF THE GOSPEL

He committed no sin, neither was deceit found in his mouth. When he was reviled, he did not revile in return; when he suffered, he did not threaten, but continued entrusting himself to him who judges justly. He himself bore our sins in his body on the tree, that we might die to sin and live to righteousness. By his wounds you have been healed. For you were straying like sheep, but have now returned to the Shepherd and Overseer of your souls (1 Peter 2:22-25).

Chapter 3

*The Sin of Anger,
and the Wrath-bearing Savior*

Why are believers not completely sanctified?
Believers are not completely or perfectly sanctified
because they retain some remnants of sin throughout their
whole being and are continually plagued with the desires of
their old sinful nature that are contrary to the spirit.
(Romans 7:18; Mark 14:66-72; Galatians 2:11-12)

THE LARGER CATECHISM in Modern English, #78[1]

Now this I say and testify in the Lord, that you must
no longer walk as the Gentiles do, in the futility
of their minds. They are darkened in their understanding, alienated from the life of God because of
the ignorance that is in them, due to their hardness
of heart. They have become callous and have given
themselves up to sensuality, greedy to practice every
kind of impurity. But that is not the way you learned
Christ! — assuming that you have heard about him
and were taught in him, as the truth is in Jesus, to

put off your old self, which belongs to your former manner of life and is corrupt through deceitful desires, and to be renewed in the spirit of your minds, and to put on the new self, created after the likeness of God in true righteousness and holiness. Therefore, having put away falsehood, let each one of you speak the truth with his neighbor, for we are members one of another. Be angry and do not sin; do not let the sun go down on your anger, and give no opportunity to the devil. Let the thief no longer steal, but rather let him labor, doing honest work with his own hands, so that he may have something to share with anyone in need. Let no corrupting talk come out of your mouths, but only such as is good for building up, as fits the occasion, that it may give grace to those who hear. And do not grieve the Holy Spirit of God, by whom you were sealed for the day of redemption. Let all bitterness and wrath and anger and clamor and slander be put away from you, along with all malice. Be kind to one another, tenderhearted, forgiving one another, as God in Christ forgave you. Therefore be imitators of God, as beloved children. And walk in love, as Christ loved us and gave himself up for us, a fragrant offering and sacrifice to God (Ephesians 4:17 – 5:2).

It is hard and unpleasant work for us to look at ourselves and see our sins. It is much easier and much more enjoyable to point out and to comment upon the sins of others! But pointing out and commenting upon the sins of others really does us very little good, if any, and much more likely does damage to our own souls. Therefore, the Lord requires us to do the hard work of dealing with our own sins, our individual sins, individually.[2] Here's a great quote along these lines from a great Puritan spiritual doctor, John Owen (1616-1683): "Be killing sin, or sin will be killing you."[3]

That's true of all sins, but it seems perhaps especially true of anger. Anger is that sin, or sinful disposition, which most often moves us to violate the sixth commandment, "You shall not murder" (Exodus 20:13). In the Sermon on the Mount, Jesus made it clear that anger in the heart is murder in the heart (Matthew 5:22). And if we don't kill this sinful disposition in us, then surely this sinful disposition will kill us. It will either burn you up with high blood pressure or take you down in depression. And that's just physiological and psychological. The spiritual side effects are much worse. Bitterness, resentment, vindictiveness – these are the weeds which spring from the seeds of anger, and they will choke all of the joy and happiness and pleasure out of your life. Anger will kill the relationships which God intended to be most meaningful and fulfilling in your life.

Anger can be a dangerously deceptive emotion. The reason for this is that, by God's design, anger is part of a physiological response intended to aid us in self-defense or self-preservation. In moments when anger flashes, our brain releases chemicals such as adrenaline and cortisol so that our heart rate increases, eyes dilate, etc., and we are enabled to run faster and jump higher and perform feats of great physical strength in order to protect or preserve our physical life. The problem for us these days is that, most often, when we flash with anger, we are usually *not* in a life-threatening situation. Our brain is telling us that our life is endangered, but in reality it isn't – at least not physically – and so we are deceived into thinking that we must react in a manner driven by anger.

Anger can be a dangerously deceptive emotion. When I am angry, I think I am right, and I think that I'm in the right. Is that true of you? *And the angrier I get, the righter I get,* at least in my mind. Let's say, for example, that you did something that offended me, that made me mad. *Well, then, don't I have a "right" to be angry, and am I not "in the right" in* *my anger, and isn't the degree of my anger an indication of the degree of my rightness against your offense?*

Probably not. Because (truth be told) you probably did not offend me; you probably offended my pride, my *sinful* pride. And you didn't *make* me mad. I *chose* to get mad. I *chose* to take offense because I felt that you had threatened my sovereign lordship over the universe. And so to defend and protect my "rights" in my self-centered world where I sit upon my throne, I chose to attack you with anger in order to drive you out of my presence.

Anger can be a dangerously deceptive emotion because it blinds us to our own sins. Anger defends our self-centeredness. Anger promotes our self-righteousness. Anger protects our sinful pride. Anger fights for our selfish desires. And it does so all the while furthering our delusion that we are without sin.

But, by God's grace, anger can also further our self-understanding and spiritual transformation. Instead of focusing on the external stimuli, we can look within and pay attention to what's going on inside of us. Underneath anger, giving rise to anger, are two deeper emotions or realities: *pain* or *fear*, or both. The next time my anger flashes, I need to step back, take a deep breath, and ask myself the questions, *"What am I afraid of in this situation?"* and/or *"Where does it hurt? Why is this situation causing me pain?"*

What am I afraid of, and how am I going to deal with that fear, whatever it is? What does the Bible say?

When I am afraid,
I put my trust in you (Psalm 56:3);
Even though I walk through the valley of the shadow of death, I will fear no evil (Psalm 23:4);
The LORD is my light and my salvation.
Whom shall I fear? (Psalm 27:1).

What do we do with those fears? What is the antidote to the fear that underlies our anger? The antidote is to trust in the sovereign God who rules over the universe and cares for my life with perfect goodness and wisdom: "...for God gave us a spirit not of fear, but of power and love and self-control" (2 Timothy 1:7).

And, *"Where does it hurt? Why is this situation causing me pain?"*

These are important questions to ask. The hurt is real. What are you going to do with that pain? You have a Savior who was "...despised and rejected by men, a man of sorrows, and acquainted with grief ..." (Isaiah 53:3). You have a glorified Savior in heaven, at the right hand of God the Father, who has not forgotten what it is like to suffer. Through faith in Jesus Christ, we have a God of all comfort who comforts us in all our affliction (2 Corinthians 1:4). When you hurt, will you go to him?

Now, you may want to ask about *righteous* anger, *righteous* indignation. Righteous indignation has to do with situations, circumstances, and events in which God's honor is violated and God's law is broken; that's the basis for *righteous* indignation. And, yes, Jesus, the sinless Son of God, on various occasions expressed righteous indignation, and he acted sinlessly with righteous indignation. And, as for us, yes, we can be angry about an injustice, angry about the fact that the law of God has been violated. As the Scripture says, we are to "abhor evil" (Romans 12:9). And in that sense, we can feel a kind of "righteous indignation" when we witness the dishonoring of God or the violation of his law. And, yes, sometimes we ourselves or those we know and love will suffer due to a sinful deed committed against us, or will suffer because of an injustice perpetrated throughout the society in which we live, or suffer a personal violation as the victim of criminal activity. In those cases, the anger which arises within us is not only understandable but also justifiable; this is "righteous anger."

But that does *not* mean that every word or deed motivated by righteous indignation is necessarily righteous and justifiable. If I act or speak when my anger is *in control of me*, if personal anger is the primary motivation and "energy source" for my words or deeds, if anger is driving the reaction to my pain, then it is highly unlikely and perhaps impossible that I will be acting sinlessly with righteous indignation. Let us not deceive ourselves about our anger in every situation being "righteous anger." To put it bluntly, it may be rare that you and I have purely righteous anger in our day-to-day experience; and even when our anger is justifiable, we must be very careful not to act or react in sinful ways to the situation.

And at this point, I want to make a connection with what's going on in our nation today.[4] In the midst of this national and global economic crisis, the anger is rising. The media loves to display this anger as a way to capture our attention and increase their ratings: two talking heads on the divided screen screaming at each other. Beware: Do not feed on the toxic anger of our popular culture. Do not imbibe, do not drink in, the toxic anger of our culture. When you're listening to the radio, or watching the news, and you're hearing all the angry commentary about what's going wrong in America, and it gets all those chemicals churning around in your brain, and you feel yourself getting angrier and angrier and angrier, remember: Be "...slow to anger, for the anger of man does not produce the righteousness God requires" (James 1:20).

That's at least one of the reasons that Ephesians 4:26 says, "Be angry and do not sin." That's a direct quote of Psalm 4:4, a psalm which cries out against lying and slander. So the context is that of "righteous indignation," but nevertheless it says, "Be angry and do not sin." Even when our anger is truly justified (and, yes, sometimes it is), even then we had better make sure that we are not acting in sinful anger, controlled by our anger and driven by irrational rage because, if so, we will surely sin.

In his commentary on Ephesians 4:26, John Calvin has some very insightful pastoral guidance to give. Calvin says that we go astray with regard to anger in three ways. First, we sin when "our anger arises from slight causes, and often from no cause whatsoever, or at least from private [personal] injuries and offenses."[5] In other words, we sin with anger when we take offense too easily, when we're so overly concerned with ourselves and so hypersensitive about ourselves that we become angry about every little misstep anyone ever makes toward us. Proverbs 19:11 says,

> Good sense makes one slow to anger,
> and it is his glory to overlook an offense.

I remember a theology professor who once commented, "It is a sign of Christian maturity not to give offense; but it is a sign of greater maturity in Christ not to *take* offense." It really ought not to surprise us too terribly much when an unbelieving pagan is rude to us; and it ought not to surprise us too terribly much when even our own brother or sister in Christ stumbles and steps on our toes. I've probably stepped on a few toes myself without intending it or knowing it; *how about you?*

The second way we go astray with regard to anger, says Calvin, is "...when we go beyond proper bounds and are hurried into intemperate excess."[6] In other words, there are times when we just need to get a grip; it's really no big deal! But anger, when it gets swirling around in our brains, has a way of magnifying the situation, and then our reactions get blown-up out of all proportion. Then we lash out with hurtful words and act out with sinful deeds. You may know the quotable quote which goes like this:

"Speak when you are angry, and you will make the best speech you will ever regret."[7] *I'm really good at that.* I can personally attest to the truth of that statement. *How about you?* But our anger is no excuse. Lack of self-control is itself a sin.

Thirdly, says Calvin, we sin when "our anger, which ought to have been directed against ourselves or against sins, is turned against our brothers."[8] In other words, we sin when in our anger we shift the blame away from ourselves to someone else. In anger, we see others' sins, but not our own sins. In anger, we want to rip the speck out of our brother's eye, but we are blind to the beam in our own eye. Whenever I in anger blame someone else for what's wrong in my life, I had better be careful to examine myself and confess my own sins which contributed to the mess.

So how do we deal with our anger? If you see someone do something which is sinful, be angry about the sin but not angry at the person. You do not need to attack the person.[9] Remember to examine yourself, and not to react in anger. If you take a deep breath, and call to mind the kindness and gentleness and forbearance with which Christ has dealt with you, then you can make a distinction between the sin and the sinner, and act in a more appropriate, godly manner.

There is another important spiritual discipline which we are to learn from the second half of Ephesians 4:26; "...do not let the sun go down on your anger." That's some of the best marriage counseling that I could give to any couple. Don't go to bed mad. Bring it to resolution. Be reconciled to one another through humble confession and genuine forgiveness. But of course this verse is not only for married couples; it's for us all. And it's some of the best pastoral counseling that I could give to anyone. Don't stew. Don't nurse the grudge. Don't go to bed thinking about how angry you are, and wake up "on the wrong side of the bed." When anger controls you, you are being controlled by the person or situation involved in the conflict. You think that anger gives you power, but it doesn't. Anger saps your power; anger takes whatever power you have and turns it in on you in self-destructive ways.

Sinful anger is death-dealing, and here's the reason why, straight from Scripture: sinful anger gives an opportunity to the devil (Ephesians 4:27). When we hold on to anger, when we do not let go, when we let anger get its grip on us, we give an opportunity to the devil. He can set the hook of anger in our hearts and jerk us around and reel us in whenever and wherever and however he wants. If the devil has set the hook of anger in your heart, and he's got you on his line, cut it! Anger can be a powerfully deceptive emotion, and the devil will use it to deceive you in an attempt to destroy you.

That is the reason that God's word says, "Let all bitterness and wrath and anger and clamor and slander be put away from you, along with all malice" (Ephesians 4:31). That kind of sinful, vindictive anger is toxic to your soul, toxic to your relationships, toxic to the Body of Christ, and is completely contradictory to a profession of faith in Jesus Christ – *completely contradictory to a profession of faith in Jesus Christ.*

If your heart is filled with anger toward someone, if your soul is hardened with ill-will against someone, if your inner spirit will not rest until that other person has "got what's coming to him"; if you play the scene over and over in your mind, finding yet another reason to resent the other person and imagine your revenge; if you will not let go of the hurt (real hurt, but you won't let go of it); if you enjoy the misery of having been wronged and offended, if your bad feeling of anger feels *good*: Beware of your anger, and heed the warning of Jesus Christ, who said, "...if you do not forgive others their trespasses, neither will your Father forgive your trespasses" (Matthew 6:15). *Jesus said it.*

If you are completely unwilling to show kindness and mercy and forgiveness toward someone who has wronged you, and your wrath has not been turned away from that person, then that may very well be evidence that in fact you have never experienced and received the grace and mercy of God through Jesus Christ – even if you claim to be a Christian. Now, we are getting to the heart of the matter.

I want you to think about this with me. We take offenses and wrongs against ourselves pretty seriously, don't we? And when we're angry, we take our anger pretty seriously, don't we? But how do we compare the wrongs that are done against us with the wrongs that we have done against *God*? How do others' wrongs against us compare to our wrongs against the infinite and eternal Holy One? There is no comparison! We should be much more grieved by *our offenses against God* than by others' offenses against us.

Do we think that we have a "right" to take our sinful anger seriously? Then what about God's right to take *his* righteous anger seriously? There it is: When you are tempted to act in anger, when you feel the impulse to rail and rant and attack in anger, when you are angered by someone's offense against you, just think about your sins against God, your offenses against the infinite and eternal Almighty One, and contemplate the righteous wrath of the Holy One whom you have offended.

And now, see the consequences of your sins against God! Where do you see those horrible consequences? Look to the cross, and see the righteous wrath of God against you, poured out instead on Jesus Christ!

Jesus Christ is the wrath-bearing Savior. He, the sinless Son of God, bore the righteous wrath of his Father against your sins as your substitute in your place. He is the only One who can save you from your sins of anger, because *he suffered the righteous anger of the Holy One against your sins of anger*. In love, Jesus offered himself up as a fragrant offering, an atoning sacrifice, the sacrifice which absorbed the wrath of God against you, and turned the wrath of God away from you, so that you might receive the kindness and mercy and forgiveness of God.

And if you have received such mercy and kindness and forgiveness from God, how can you withhold it from others? If Christ has borne the righteous anger of the Almighty against my sins, then how can I dare to pour out my sinful anger upon those who have offended me?

Rather, you and I are called to be "imitators of God" who, instead of pouring out his righteous wrath upon us, has forgiven us our sins through the wrath-bearing Savior, Jesus Christ, who "loved us and gave himself up for us" (Ephesians 5:1). **He is our righteous wrath-bearing Savior.** He died under the righteous wrath of God, so that our sinful anger might be put to death. Therefore, let all wrath and anger be put away from us; and may we, in union with Jesus Christ through faith, by the power of the Holy Spirit, forgive one another as God in Christ has forgiven us, and "walk in love as Christ loved us" (Ephesians 4:31 – 5:2).

For Further Meditation and Spiritual Exercise

A CALL TO CONFESSION

Jesus said, "I say to you that everyone who is angry with his brother will be liable to the judgment" (Matthew 5:22).

A man of wrath stirs up strife,
and one given to anger causes much transgression (Proverbs 29:22).

Let all bitterness and wrath and anger and clamor and slander be put away from you, along with all malice (Ephesians 4:31).

Let every person be quick to hear, slow to speak, slow to anger; for the anger of man does not produce the righteousness that God requires (James 1:19).

A PRAYER OF CONFESSION

Have mercy upon me, O God, according to your steadfast love; according to your abundant mercy, blot out my transgressions. Wash me thoroughly from my iniquity, and cleanse me from my sin. I humbly confess:

My anger, which spews forth in hurtful words;

My anger, which seethes in hateful thoughts;

My anger, which motivates and rationalizes wrongful actions;

My anger, which falsely accuses and blames others;

My anger, which seeks revenge, if only in my imagination;

My anger, which defends my self-righteousness, and blinds me to my own sins;

My anger, which hangs on to past hurts and offenses;

My anger, which enslaves me to bitterness and resentment;

My anger, which blinds me from seeing my blessings;

My anger, which will not let me forgive others;

My anger, which prevents me from receiving forgiveness from you.

A PRAYER OF REPENTANCE AND TRANSFORMATION

Holy Father, my sinful anger does not produce the righteousness that you require. Give me the grace and power of the Holy Spirit, that I may put away all bitterness and wrath and anger and all malice. May your Holy Spirit set me free from the bondage of anger, so that I may live a life of love, being kind and tenderhearted and forgiving toward others, even as you, in Christ, have forgiven me. For I deserve your wrath, but seek your mercy through the blood of Jesus who bore your wrath for me. Amen.

THE ASSURANCE OF THE GOSPEL

For while we were still weak, at the right time Christ died for the ungodly. For one will scarcely die for a righteous person – though perhaps for a good person one would dare even to die – but God shows his love for us in that while we were still sinners, Christ died for us. Since, therefore, we have now been justified by his blood, much more shall we be saved by him from the wrath of God (Romans 5:6-9).

Chapter 4

The Sin of Sloth,
and the Ever-Working Savior

What is the dying-away of the old self?
It is to be genuinely sorry for sin, to hate
it more and more, and to run away from it.

What is the coming-to-life of the new self?
It is wholehearted joy in God through Christ and
a delight to do every kind of good as God wants us to.
(Psalm 51:3-4, 17; Joel 2:12-13; Romans 8:12-13; 2 Corinthians 7:10)

THE HEIDELBERG CATECHISM, #89-90[1]

For by the grace given to me I say to everyone
among you not to think of himself more highly than
he ought to think, but to think with sober judgment,
each according to the measure of faith that God has
assigned. For as in one body we have many members, and the members do not all have the same func-
tion, so we, though many, are one body in Christ, and
individually members one of another. Having gifts

that differ according to the grace given to us, let us use them: if prophecy, in proportion to our faith; if service, in our serving; the one who teaches, in his teaching; the one who exhorts, in his exhortation; the one who contributes, in generosity; the one who leads, with zeal; the one who does acts of mercy, with cheerfulness. Let love be genuine. Abhor what is evil; hold fast to what is good. Love one another with brotherly affection. Outdo one another in showing honor. Do not be slothful in zeal, be fervent in spirit, serve the Lord. Rejoice in hope, be patient in tribulation, be constant in prayer. Contribute to the needs of the saints and seek to show hospitality (Romans 12:3-13).

The fourth of "the seven deadly sins" is the sin (or sinful disposition) of **sloth**. But right away, I want to make it clear: There's a big difference between being unwilling to work (sloth) and being unable to find employment in today's economy.[2]

This nation is undergoing an economic crisis of historic proportions. Unemployment is on the rise. Due to no fault of their own, many otherwise hardworking people are currently unemployed. That is a heavy burden to bear, not only financially but also psychologically, emotionally, and spiritually. Nothing in this chapter is intended to add to that burden. To the contrary, as the church of Jesus Christ, the "communion of saints," the fellowship of believers, we are called to bear one another's burdens: personally, spiritually, and, if need be, to the degree that God enables us, materially and financially. If we as the Body of Christ do not do what we *can* do to help bear one another's burdens, then we ourselves will be guilty of *sloth*.

The passage from Romans 12 may not seem like a text related to the sin of sloth because we probably most often think of sloth in terms of physical laziness, shiftlessness, and unwillingness to work, usually related to "employment" or physical labor such as "housework" or "chores" on the "to do" list. And, yes, sloth does relate to those things (more about that later), but we also need to understand that sloth is a deeply spiritual issue which affects *every* area of our life and which needs to be rooted out of every area of our life. Romans 12:1 says, "...present your bodies as a living sacrifice," calling us to offer the totality of our lives into the service of God, "which is your spiritual worship." That is a call to an actively engaged (not slothful) life of Christian discipleship. The passage then specifies some practical applications of that general exhortation, teaching us to serve the church with our spiritual gifts for the building up of the Body. What's the point? We see the clear connection here in this passage: In response to the mercies of God, we offer ourselves as living sacrifices to God, seeking the transformation of our lives by the renewal of our minds (Romans 12:2) for the sake of service in the Body of Christ (Romans 12:3-8); and that service is to be offered with *generosity, zeal* and *cheerfulness* – the opposites of sloth (Romans 12:8).

But beyond service in the Body of Christ, the Scripture also calls us to nurture personal relationships with one another in the church, and to nurture the spiritual life within us individually and among us corporately. And so, the Scripture says,

> Let love be genuine. Abhor what is evil; hold fast to what is good. Love one another with brotherly affection. Outdo one another in showing honor. Do not be slothful in zeal, be fervent in spirit, serve the Lord. Rejoice in hope, be patient in tribulation, be constant in prayer. Contribute to the needs of the saints and seek to show hospitality (Romans 12:9-13).

I hope you can feel the energy in those exhortations. As believers who have been redeemed by the mercies of God through the blood of Jesus Christ, we are called to live out our faith energetically, enthusiastically, and wholeheartedly. There's nothing lazy about the Christian life. Right in the middle of these exhortations is the command, "Do not be slothful in zeal" (Romans 12:11). There's the warning against sloth. But in this context it's not directly related to "employment" or "housework" or other types of "work." It's a warning against *spiritual sloth*. Don't be slothful in your love for one another. Don't be slothful in abhorring evil. Don't be slothful in holding fast to what is good. Don't be slothful in showing honor to one another. Don't be slothful in your daily witness; don't grow cold; don't give up hope; don't lose your joy; don't be slothful in prayer. The Christian life is to be lived with the energy that the Spirit of God supplies. *There's nothing lazy about the Christian faith.*

In his letter to the Philippians, the Apostle Paul put it this way:

> ...work out your own salvation with fear and trembling, for it is God who works in you, both to will and to work for his good pleasure (Philippians 2:12-13).

In other words, God, who is the source of your salvation, is also the source of your sanctification, your transformation; so, by the power of his Spirit at work in you, work it out, live it out. *There's nothing lazy about the Christian life.* "Do not be slothful in zeal" (Romans 12:11).

This theme of fervency, zeal, and energy in faith (the opposite of spiritual sloth) runs throughout the New Testament. To the Colossians, Paul wrote:

...I *toil*, struggling with all his [Christ's] energy that he powerfully works in me (Colossians 1:29; emphasis and insertion mine).

Concerning the work of the gospel, the Apostle Paul wrote to Timothy,

...to this end we *toil* and *strive*, because we have our hope set on the living God (1 Timothy 4:10, emphasis mine).

At the conclusion of the great fifteenth chapter of First Corinthians, the chapter on the victory of Christ's resurrection over death, and the promise of our resurrection from the dead, Paul exclaims, "Thanks be to God, who gives us the victory through our Lord Jesus Christ" (1 Corinthians 15:58). But he doesn't stop there. And he doesn't say, *"Therefore, since Christ has won the victory and he gives it to us, all we do now is wait for him to take us to heaven." No!* To the contrary, he says,

Therefore, my beloved, be steadfast, immovable, always abounding in the work of the Lord, knowing that in the Lord your labor is not in vain (1 Corinthians 15:58).

That is an anti-sloth exhortation!

The Christian life cannot be lived lazily, listlessly, shiftlessly, carelessly, and apathetically. And since every aspect of our lives is to be devoted to the glory of God, then everything we do should be characterized by this spiritual zeal. Colossians 3:17 says, "Whatever you do, in word or deed, do all in the name of the Lord Jesus, giving thanks to God the

Father through him." Therefore, we are warned against sloth in all its forms in every area of our life.

The book of Proverbs is filled with warnings against sloth. But underneath the warnings against sloth, there is a very important theological point: The God we meet in the Bible is not a derelict deity. He is a God who works tirelessly, with mighty power, amazing creativity and intentional purpose; and he is a God who delights in his works! You and I were created in his image and likeness to reflect his glory as we work vigorously in his world (Genesis 1:27; 2:15). We were never intended to be idle, slothful oafs, not even in Paradise! Before Adam had ever sinned, the LORD had already put him in the Garden of Eden "to work it and keep it" (Genesis 2:15). God always intended for us to be *workers*: to have responsibilities, to fulfill duties, to employ our intellectual and physical strengths in service to him in this world. And in heaven, the glorified saints and angels serve the Holy One with joyful zeal and energy! *There is no sloth in heaven!*

But now, because of our sinful nature, sloth corrupts us. Sloth mars and defaces the image of God in us. That's what's wrong with sloth: It is *ungodly*. Sloth is an expression of our sinful nature.

How do we address the sloth in our life? What about how we do our work at our place of employment or in the home? For children and youth, this would include their schoolwork, which is one of their primary areas of work at this time in their lives, along with any household chores and responsibilities they may have. All the Scriptural admonitions apply: "Whatever you do, work heartily, as for the Lord and not for men" (Colossians 3:23). Why? Because, the Scripture says, "You are serving the Lord Christ" (Colossians 3:24). Why work heartily? Because, whatever you are doing, wherever you work, "you are serving the Lord Christ" in his world for his glory!

This biblical attitude is in direct contrast to the ungodly view of work, which says, *"It's a job. It pays the bills. And, just like everybody else, I'll do what I have to, as little as possible, to get by, and hope to get as much out of it as I possibly can."*

That is an attitude of sloth, and it is an ugly offense to God.

Sloth now has a great promoter in the "wonderful world" of the Internet and instant communication. How much time do you think is wasted in workplaces in America, with employees "surfing the Web," sending personal emails, or playing solitaire on their computers? It's sloth; sloth at your fingertips, sloth satisfied by the click of a mouse. The way you do your work – honestly, industriously, heartily, energetically, reliably, cheerfully, to the best of your ability, "as to the Lord and not to man" (Ephesians 6:7) – that's the foundation which establishes the integrity of your Christian witness in the workplace; and without that foundation of good, honest work, anything you say about Christ, anything you say about the Christian faith, will be cast in the negative light of your poor personal example at work.

But what about the important work that takes place in our homes? Parents, are we teaching our children to share household responsibilities cheerfully? The way we do that is not to nag them but to model for them the cheerful doing of our own household duties. Are we modeling to our children that we all have to do things that we do not *feel* like doing? *Feelings are a wonderful thing to "get over."* Dare I ask how much time is wasted in your home (dare I ask how much time *I waste*) with the trivialities – the inane, the idiotic, the good-for-nothing trivialities – of the Internet? In terms of time-management priorities, it's no longer a matter of the "tyranny of the urgent"; no, it's tyranny – *tyranny!* – of the *trivial!* There's a word for it, and the word is **sloth**, and it is sin.

Sloth is not merely a matter of "sleeping late." Sloth is not merely a matter of "shiftlessness," laziness in the stereotypical definition. **Sloth is also the sinful inclination to avoid the most important things in life.** Sloth loves trivial distractions that keep us from doing what we really should be doing. It's funny that we might think that we're not guilty of sloth, that sloth is not really an issue in our lives, because we're all so ... *busy*! But the truth is: *Busyness* is a form of sloth. Sloth loves to be busy doing lots of unimportant things, as an excuse to avoid doing the really important things that God calls and commands us to do.

It takes time and energy – work, commitment, effort – to nurture a marriage, to cultivate a happy and holy home, to raise children in the discipline and instruction of the Lord. Those things don't just happen; and they won't happen if we dabble around with them only when we "feel" like it. But sloth is the excuse that says we're too busy, or we're too tired, or we're too *this* or too *that*, to do the most important things and fulfill the most important responsibilities of our life.

"Husbands, love your wives, as Christ loved the church and gave himself up for her" (Ephesians 5:25). There's nothing slothful about that. "And let the wife see that she respects her husband" (Ephesians 5:33). There's nothing slothful about that. "Fathers, do not provoke your children to anger, but bring them up in the discipline and instruction of the Lord" (Ephesians 6:4). No room for sloth there.

And there is no room for sloth when we look specifically at the spiritual disciplines of the Christian life. How often do we recognize the sin of prayerlessness for what it really is? **Prayerlessness is a sin which arises largely out of sloth.** True prayer is real work. Prayer requires the engagement of our minds, our hearts, our souls, our emotions, our will. Prayer requires our attention. If we want real communion with God, we will have to do more than offer those "off the top of our head" prayers as we're flitting through our "busy lives."

What is it that keeps us from blocking out twenty or thirty minutes a day, with no telephone (no cell phone!), no television, no email, no Internet, no wireless gizmo, in order to sit still in silence and solitude in prayer? It's not that we don't have the time; it's *sloth* that keeps us from that communion with God, because sitting still in silence and solitude and focusing our hearts and concentrating our minds on the presence of the Holy One is "hard work." We'd rather be "busy." We'd rather be *doing something*, mindlessly. We'd rather have the room filled up with noise, with our minds flitting elsewhere, than to concentrate our hearts and minds upon the presence of God. We need to realize it, recognize it, name it – *sloth* – and crucify it!

What is it that keeps us from coming to worship on the Lord's Day with joy and expectation in our hearts, with minds awake and souls energetically eager to worship the Lord and feed upon his word in fellowship with his people? What keeps us from that? *Sloth*: spiritual apathy. It's just easier to go through the motions, and to watch what happens in worship and to evaluate it according to our personal tastes rather than to engage in the worship of the living God, with heart and soul and mind and strength. Proverbs 13:4 says,

> The soul of the sluggard craves and gets nothing,
> while the soul of the diligent is richly supplied.

Proverbs 26:15 speaks in a very insightful imagery:

> The sluggard buries his hand in the dish;
> it wears him out to bring it back to his mouth.

These proverbs apply not only to economic realities but also to spiritual realities. The soul of the sluggard craves spiritual blessings and gets nothing, while the soul of the diligent is richly supplied. Are we diligent in prayer? Are we diligent in the study of the Scripture? Are we diligent in the application of the Bible to our lives? Are we diligent in observing the means of grace – worship on the Lord's Day, hearing God's word proclaimed, examining ourselves, confessing our sins, renewing our covenant with Christ at his Table? The soul of the diligent is richly supplied. But the spiritual sluggard is like the man who dips his hand in the dish, but is too lazy to bring it back to his mouth (Proverbs 26:15). He sits down to a feast, but never eats!

Are you feasting on the word of God in personal study, or is your Bible collecting dust on the shelf? Are you feasting in corporate worship, singing praise from your heart? Or are you only mouthing the words? Are you feasting on the preached word, even when it's convicting you of your sin? Or are you wondering when it's going to be over? Your hand is in the dish, but are you feasting? *Do not be slothful in zeal.*

There is still another kind of sloth to address. The Scripture says, "abhor what is evil" (Romans 12:9). There is a kind of moral sloth which is apathetic about the evils, injustices, wrongs, and sufferings in this world. To sit back, concerned mainly with our own creature comforts, as long as evils and ills such as abortion, infanticide, genocide, sex trafficking, religious persecution, world hunger, and homelessness continue to mar God's creation (until Christ comes again!), is to be guilty of *moral sloth.* And to say that we can't really make a difference because the problem is too big, or the problem is too complicated, or the problem is too controversial and it would be best not to get involved, so that we end up doing nothing – that is what the *sluggard* says. Proverbs 22:13 puts it like this:

The sluggard says, "There is a lion outside!
I shall be killed in the streets!"

The point is: A moral sluggard is a moral coward; and a moral coward is a moral sluggard. ***Do not be slothful in zeal.***

Now, when I look at my life in this light, I see sloth and the need to crucify it. How about you? But how do we crucify sloth? How do we fan the flame, how do we remain fervent in spirit? This spiritual zeal does not reside within us by means of our own resources. No. This spiritual zeal comes only through the presence of the ever-working Savior in our lives. **He, Jesus Christ, is the One who never became slothful in zeal.** It was zeal for his Father's will which empowered him to live a life of perfect obedience. It was zeal for his Father's will which moved him to become obedient unto death, even death on a cross. It was spiritual zeal, zealous love, which moved him to give himself up for us on the cross. **Only Jesus Christ can save and deliver us from the sins of sloth because only Jesus Christ is the ever-working Savior.** On the cross, he *worked* a wonderful redemption for us! In his resurrection from the dead, he *worked* a mighty salvation for us! In his ascension into heaven, he *worked* a glorious triumph for us! And now at the right hand of the Father, he *works* for us as our Advocate, Intercessor, and Mediator.

He never stops working for us! He never neglects his responsibilities toward us! The Scripture says that Jesus Christ, at the right hand of God the Father Almighty

> …holds his priesthood permanently, because he con-
> tinues forever. Consequently, he is able to save to the
> uttermost those who draw near to God through him,
> since he always lives to make intercession for them
> (Hebrews 7:24-25).

Jesus Christ never ever becomes slothful in zeal! That's the kind of Savior he is: ***the ever-working Savior!***

Look to him! Receive from him the forgiveness of all your sins of sloth! Receive from him the power to be delivered from the slavery to sloth! Receive from him the mighty power of the Holy Spirit, so that you, with thanksgiving and joy and courage and peace, may be fervent in spirit, serving the Lord, ***never slothful in zeal!***

For Further Meditation and Spiritual Exercise

A CALL TO CONFESSION

The soul of the sluggard craves and gets nothing, while the soul of the diligent is richly supplied (Proverbs 13:4).

How long will you lie there, O sluggard?
When will you arise from your sleep?
A little sleep, a little slumber, a little folding of the hands to rest, and poverty will come upon you like a robber, and want like an armed man (Proverbs 6:9-11).

The sluggard buries his hand in the dish; it wears him out to bring it back to his mouth (Proverbs 26:15).

The sluggard does not plow in the autumn; he will seek at harvest and have nothing (Proverbs 20:4).

A PRAYER OF CONFESSION

Almighty and most merciful Father, I acknowledge and confess that I have sinned against you, not only by the things that I have done but also by not doing what I should have done. In your mercy, through the work of Christ on the cross for me, forgive my sins of sloth:

My sloth, which resists the fulfilling of my daily responsibilities and duties;

My sloth, which expects others to take care of my needs;

My sloth, which neglects the needs of others;

My sloth, which does not give an honest day's work for an honest day's pay;

My sloth, which wastes time in distracting trivialities;

My sloth, which would prefer to sleep than to pray;

My sloth, which prefers mindless television over thoughtful reading;

My sloth, which prefers spoon-fed tidbits over the meat of your word;

My sloth, which prefers entertainment over worship;

My sloth, which is apathetic about the injustices and wrongs in the world;

My sloth, which makes excuses for not attempting to deal with difficult issues;

My sloth, which keeps me "busy" in my activities, but slow to do your will;

My sloth, which tolerates and excuses the sin in my life;

My sloth, which hinders me from serving you with zeal and joy.

A PRAYER OF REPENTANCE AND TRANSFORMATION

Gracious Father, I give you thanks that you are not a slothful deity, but a God who works mightily by the power of your word and Spirit through your Son, Jesus Christ. I give you thanks and praise for the great work of salvation which he wrought by his death on the cross and his resurrection from the grave. I give you thanks for his continuing work of intercession and mediation for me at your right hand. I give you thanks for the work of the

Holy Spirit in me, that I might have new and everlasting life in union with Christ. Continue your work in me, O God, that by the power of your Spirit I might work out my salvation with fear and trembling! Grant me the grace and the power to press on toward the goal for the prize of the upward call in Christ Jesus, and to run with endurance the race that is set before me. Renew my mind and transform my life; deliver me from the inclinations and habits of sloth, so that I might be fervent in spirit, serving you, bearing fruit in every good work; to the glory of your holy name. Amen.

THE ASSURANCE OF THE GOSPEL

Oh sing to the LORD a new song,
for he has done marvelous things!
His right hand and his holy arm
have worked salvation for him (Psalm 98:1).

...the Son of Man came not to be served but to serve, and to give his life as a ransom for many (Mark 10:45).

My little children, I am writing these things to you so that you may not sin. But if anyone does sin, we have an advocate with the Father, Jesus Christ the righteous (1 John 2:1).

... he [Jesus Christ] holds his priesthood permanently, because he continues forever. Consequently, he is able to save to the uttermost those who draw near to God through him, since he always lives to make intercession for them (Hebrews 7:24-25, insertion mine).

Chapter 5

The Sin of Greed, and the Impoverished Savior

Just as there is no sin so small that it does not deserve damnation, so there is no sin so great that it can bring damnation upon those who truly repent.

THE WESTMINSTER CONFESSION OF FAITH
in Modern English[1]

Do you not know that the unrighteous will not inherit the kingdom of God? Do not be deceived: neither the sexually immoral, nor idolaters, nor adulterers, nor men who practice homosexuality, nor thieves, nor the greedy, nor drunkards, nor revilers, nor swindlers will inherit the kingdom of God. And such were some of you. But you were washed, you were sanctified, you were justified in the name of the Lord Jesus Christ and by the Spirit of our God (1 Corinthians 6:9-11).

Given the economic turmoil our nation is experiencing, it is an interesting time to address the sin of greed.[2] Perhaps it is *timely*. But before I deal directly with the sin of greed, I want to look at the positive, godly, Biblical teaching concerning money. **The sin, or sinful disposition, of greed is a corruption and perversion of the good, Biblical attitude toward wealth.**

That is an important spiritual principle for us to understand about sin. The inclinations of our sinful nature and all of our actual sins are corruptions and perversions of something which is good. What is a rotten apple? A rotten apple is a good apple that has gone bad. That's the way sin works in our lives. It takes something good in its essence, such as wealth (earthly, material blessing) and perverts, corrupts, and ruins it, so that what ought to produce gratitude instead produces greed.

Let's begin in the very beginning. After God had created his good and beautiful and bountiful world, he "saw everything that he had made, and behold, it was very good" (Genesis 1:30). And he said to the man and woman, "Behold, I have given you every plant yielding seed that is on the face of all the earth, and every tree with seed in its fruit. You shall have them for food" (Genesis 1:29). God had made everything, and then he gave everything – unspoiled, uncorrupted, in all its beauty and bounty – freely to the man and the woman. The creation was God's gift to his human creatures.

Let me ask you: Were they wealthy? You bet they were. Where did their wealth come from? From God's sovereign, free grace. Who was the source of their wealth? God. Was there anything sinful about the fact that they lived in a world of plenty with all of their needs supplied? Not at all. Was there any reason that they should have felt guilty about the bountiful provision for their lives? None at all.

What's the point? Material bounty, *in its essence*, is not sinful; it is a "good" thing in God's good creation. It reflects God's own goodness, generosity, and magnanimity (I love that word in reference to God: ***magnanimity!*** It means: extremely gracious, super-abundant, overflowing, freely-flowing ***generosity***).

But, you might say, we don't live in the Garden of Eden. We live after the fall into sin. The world is corrupted by sin. We are corrupted by sin. What about material wealth in the fallen world? Good question! What does the Bible say? The book of Deuteronomy tells us that before the Israelites entered the good land which the Lord had promised them, he spoke to them through Moses, saying,

> ...the Lord your God is bringing you into a good land, a land of brooks of water, of fountains and springs, flowing out in the valleys and hills, a land of wheat and barley, of vines and fig trees and pomegranates, a land of olive trees and honey, a land in which you will eat bread without scarcity, in which you will lack nothing, a land whose stones are iron, and out of whose hills you can dig copper. And you shall eat and be full, and you shall bless the Lord your God for the good land he has given you (Deuteronomy 8:7-10).

What does that sound like to you? It sounds like it was God's intention to bless his people not merely with material provision but with material bounty. So could there be anything *inherently* sinful about material bounty? No. This passage goes on to speak about the "good houses" in which the people would live, and the multiplication of their flocks and herds and silver and gold (Deuteronomy 8:12-13). *The multiplication of their flocks and herds and silver and gold*: What is *that*? That is the return on their investment, the growth of their capital. Have you ever thought about that? The Bible has something good to say about economic growth under the blessings of God. In fact, this passage goes on to say that "it is [the LORD your God] who gives you power to get wealth" (Deuteronomy 8:18, insertion mine). Now, if it is the LORD God who gives us power to get wealth, if it is the LORD who blesses us for the multiplication of our flocks and herds and silver and gold (or whatever our capital is), then can there be anything inherently evil or sinful about wealth itself and its production and increase? No.

So then, there is a positive, godly, Biblical perspective on material wealth. But along with all these promises of blessings, there is a warning which runs throughout this passage in Deuteronomy. The warning is, "Take care lest you forget the LORD your God" (Deuteronomy 8:11). "Beware lest you say in your heart, 'My power and the might of my hand have gotten me this wealth'" (Deuteronomy 8:17). When we forget the LORD our God and become prideful in the delusion of our self-sufficiency, and we turn away from loving the LORD our God with all our heart and our neighbor as ourselves, then our gratitude gets corrupted and turns into greed, and, as this passage concludes, we "go after other gods and serve them and worship them" (Deuteronomy 8:19), and put ourselves in the peril of perishing.

Our sinful nature and our sinful inclinations have a corrupting power within us, which corrupts the blessings which God gives to us. Greed is one of those corrupting forces. Greed imperils our souls.

Corinth was a major city in Greece, filled with pagan worship and all manner of immorality. And after hearing the gospel and professing faith in Christ, the Christians in Corinth still had their pagan baggage; the immorality of the world, residing in their sinful nature, was infiltrating the Body of Christ. The Apostle Paul had to deal with some serious issues, serious sins, in the lives of the Christians in Corinth.

And so he warned them (and the Spirit of God, speaking in this passage, warns us):

> Do you not know that the unrighteous will not inherit the kingdom of God? Do not be deceived: neither the sexually immoral, nor idolaters, nor adulterers, nor men who practice homosexuality, nor thieves, nor the *greedy*, nor drunkards, nor revilers, nor swindlers will inherit the kingdom of God. And such were some of you (1 Corinthians 6:9-10, emphasis mine).

I chose this particular passage for the chapter on greed because it's significant that the sin (or sinful disposition) of greed is listed right along with *sexual immorality, idolatry, adultery, the practice of homosexuality,* and *theft*. That ought to get our attention. It ought to get our attention that the Scripture says that those whose lives are characterized by such sins – those who persistently participate unrepentantly in such sins, those whose character is dominated by such sinful attitudes and behaviors – will not inherit the kingdom of God. And that's a warning given to professing Christians! Paul intends that to be a warning to the professing Christians in Corinth. The Holy Spirit intends that to be a warning to you and me today. Let us not deceive ourselves: Willful, persistent, unrepentant pursuit of sinful behavior is deadly. The warning is to those who do not repent, who do not turn away from their sins, who willfully persist in their sins: They will not inherit the kingdom of God. And in this passage, that warning is given to "the greedy."

But this passage also speaks clearly of the transformative process which sets us free from the bondage of sin! Paul speaks of the transforming power of the gospel when he writes: *"And such were some of you!"* (1 Corinthians 6:11, emphasis mine). There were those among the Corinthian Christians who had been saved from, delivered out of, a life characterized by sexual immorality, idolatry, the practice of homosexuality, and *greed!* The gospel had set them free, and Paul was exhorting them to continue in their life of Spirit-born freedom and not to return to the slavery of their particular sins. *The riches of redemption in Christ Jesus set us free from the clutches of greed!*

Now, what is greed? How do we define it? We need to answer those questions in light of the positive, good, biblical perspective on wealth. Is it sinfully greedy to want to be honestly and gainfully employed so that you can provide for yourself and your family? Of course not. We are commanded by God to work to earn our living (2 Thessalonians 3:12). Is it sinfully greedy to want to be successful, to want to produce wealth, and to enjoy the material blessings of life on earth? *Not necessarily.* Proverbs 10:4 says, "...the hand of the diligent makes rich."

But let us also beware of the sinful corruptions of our deceitful hearts. Jesus said, "It is easier for a camel to go through the eye of a needle than for a rich person to enter the kingdom of God" (Mark 10:25). What did Jesus mean by that? At least one thing he meant is that worldly riches have a way of getting in the way between our hearts and the kingdom of God. As Jesus said on another occasion,

> "...the cares of this world and the deceitfulness of riches and the desires for other things enter in and choke the word [the word of the gospel], and it proves unfruitful" (Mark 4:19, insertion mine).

And if the word of the gospel is unfruitful in our lives, we will not enter the kingdom of God. The Apostle Paul wrote to Timothy,

> Now there is great gain in godliness with contentment, for we brought nothing into the world, and we

cannot take anything out of the world. But if we have food and clothing, with these we will be content. But those who desire to be rich fall into temptation, into a snare, into many senseless and harmful desires that plunge people into ruin and destruction. For the love of money is a root of all kinds of evils. It is through this craving that some have wandered away from the faith and pierced themselves with many pangs (1Timothy 6:6-10).

There's the warning. "Those who desire to be rich fall into temptation, into a snare … ." So where do we cross the line? In the New Testament, there are a few different Greek words which are translated into English as "greedy" and "covetous" and "ravening," depending upon the context and the specific English translation. One Greek word sometimes translated as "greed" is also translated as *extortion* or *robbery*.[3] This tells us that at least one form of greed is characterized by an inclination or motivation to cheat, trick, or abuse others for one's own personal gain. In the Old Testament, it is called "unjust gain."

> Whoever is greedy for unjust gain troubles
> his own household,
> but he who hates bribes will live (Proverbs 15:27).

False advertising, misrepresentation of goods and services, price gouging, swindling, scamming, conning, bilking, milking, manipulation, exploitation, entrapping people in a financial commitment they can't keep, inflating the expenses which are charged to another and paid to you, padding the price, frivolous lawsuits, any way of taking unfair advantage of another for economic enrichment – these are sinful behaviors of greed. And what does that tell us? We are guilty of greed whenever we do something to enrich ourselves in a way which violates God's command to love our neighbor as ourselves. That's what makes it "unjust gain" – when we violate the law of love against our neighbor, or in any way engage in deceitful, abusive, ungodly behavior for our personal enrichment.

There are other ways that we can do that. It is not only a matter of extortion and swindling and scamming. What about the child who takes the last cookie off the plate even though he has already had two and knows that his sibling has not yet had any? That's not love; that's greed. What about spending that extra $100 at the end of the month on something you wanted for yourself without talking to your spouse about it, instead of putting it into savings as previously agreed upon? That's not love and respect; that's greed. What about keeping that $10 bill which the clerk at the cash register mistakenly gave you in change instead of a $1 bill? That's unjust gain; that's stealing; that's greed. What about using your power and influence at work to position yourself with an unfair advantage to receive special bonuses or commissions at the expense of your colleague who is just as deserving? What about manipulatively grasping at the family inheritance? What about withholding God's tithe from him?[4] That's greed.

So let's dig a little deeper. What is it that would move us to act in greed, enriching ourselves at the expense of our neighbor? Why would we do that? The Bible has another phrase which is related to greed and covetousness. It is "the love of money" (1 Timothy 6:10). Let's look at that carefully. Let's not quickly say that we don't love money. You don't have to be a miserly scrooge to be a lover of money. What is involved in love, whatever it is that we love? Love of God? Love of spouse? Love of money? Love implies a relationship: a relationship of trust; a relationship in which we find security and happiness and comfort and joy and hope. "Love of money" doesn't mean that we sit around counting our coins and kissing them all day long. "Love of money" means that, at the very personal level, at the very real, practical level, money has displaced God in our lives and has taken up the role of God in our lives. That is the reason that covetousness is called "idolatry" (Colossians 3:5). Covetousness and greed are forms of idolatry because they are expressions of trust, security, happiness, comfort, and joy in *money* or *things* instead of God.

What we're learning is not that money is a bad thing but that, as the Scripture says, we ought not to set our hope on the "uncertainty of riches" (1 Timothy 6:17), for "riches do not last forever" (Proverbs 27:24). So although it may not look like or feel like "greed" *per se*, let's do a "gut check" about our relationship with money. There's certainly nothing wrong or sinful or greedy about being concerned over what's happening in the economy. There's nothing wrong, sinful, or greedy about being concerned that your job might be at risk, or that you've already been laid off, or that your retirement fund or your investments have lost value. I'm not making light of those things and I do not in any way intend to associate guilt with the basic concerns we all have.

But how do these concerns affect your soul? Are you not as happy when you are not as wealthy? There may be times when there is not a lot to be happy about concerning the economy. But is the economy the source of your happiness? And I don't mean that glibly or naively, and I don't mean for that to sound insensitive. At the end of the day, if our happiness depends upon the economy, then we'll have to find something else to be happy about. We'll have to find our happiness in God. Can you be happy without more than enough money? Can you feel secure without more than enough money? Can enough be enough? The Apostle Paul wrote, "...if we have food and clothing, with these we will be content" (1 Timothy 6:8) – *really?*

Can we be content with what we have? Hebrews 13:5 instructs us, "Keep your life free from the love of money, and be content with what you have, for he has said, "I will never leave you nor forsake you.""

Is God's presence in your life – his goodness, his grace, his mercy, his love, his fellowship – enough to keep your life free from the love of money?

Do you believe Jesus when he says, "Take care, and be on your guard against all covetousness, for one's life does not consist in the abundance of his possessions" (Luke 12:15)?

Do you believe that? Do you believe that your life does not consist in the abundance of your possessions? Frankly, that's hard to believe (isn't it?), living in the United States of America, living in a consumer culture, living in the richest nation in the history of the world, in which *enough is never enough* and the road to happiness is always paved with *more, more,* and *more.* Do we really believe Jesus when he says, "...one's life does not consist in the abundance of his possessions"?

Well, then, in the abundance of *what* does life consist? Good question! Jesus said, "*I* came that they might have life, and have it *abundantly*" (John 10:10, emphasis mine). True life consists in the abundance of grace, mercy, peace, joy, and hope that comes through faith in Jesus Christ. Do you believe that you can have, and do have, abundant life in and through Jesus Christ – no matter what happens in the stock market? Can you even conceive of life – abundant life – happiness and joy in life, apart from the standard of living you always wanted, always had, or thought you would always have?

How highly do you value the "riches of his kindness" the "riches of his glory," the "riches of his grace," that have been freely bestowed on you? These are biblical terms (Romans 2:4; 9:23; Ephesians 1:7), and they tell us that the true and eternal riches which make us *really rich* are not found in this world. They come to us from heaven, in the man Jesus Christ. As the Apostle Paul wrote to the Corinthians, "You know the grace of our Lord Jesus Christ, that though he was rich, yet for your sake he became poor; so that you by his poverty might become rich" (2 Corinthians 8:9).

Where is your wealth? Where are your riches? If you profess to be a Christian, your wealth and riches are to be found only in a man who died poor and naked on a cross: **a man who was sold out and delivered up for the sake of unjust gain.** He was betrayed for a bribe! He was nailed to the tree for the price of thirty pieces of silver. *It was your greed and mine that nailed him there!*

Jesus Christ, the impoverished Savior, is the only One who can save you from your sins of greed, because he died on the cross as the victim of greed to be the substitutionary atoning sacrifice for your sins of greed. Jesus Christ is the only One who can deliver you from the slavery of greed – deliver you from the power of the *great green goblin* – because only Christ has all the riches of heaven to bestow upon you, to fill up that empty hole in your soul.

Look to him who came that you might have life and have it abundantly! Look to him who became poor – to him who gave up the glories of heaven for the destitution of the cross – so that you might inherit the riches of heaven as a child of God. In Christ, you have "an inheritance that is imperishable, undefiled, and unfading, kept in heaven for you ..." (1 Peter 1:4). Isn't that better than anything this world can offer you? The promise of the gospel provides the power, the hope, the joy that sets us free from the slavery of greed and enables us to live gratefully, humbly, generously, and happily — even *magnanimously!* – praising God from whom all blessings flow!

For Further Meditation and Spiritual Exercise

A CALL TO CONFESSION
A greedy man stirs up strife,
but the one who trusts in the Lord will be enriched
(Proverbs 28:25).

Do not be deceived: neither the sexually immoral, nor
idolaters, nor adulterers, nor men who practice homosexuality, nor thieves, nor the greedy, nor drunkards, nor
revilers, nor swindlers will inherit the kingdom of God
(1 Corinthians 6:9-10).

For the wicked boasts of the desires of his soul,
and the one greedy for gain curses and renounces the
Lord (Psalm 10:3).

A PRAYER OF CONFESSION
Almighty Father, from your hand comes every good
and perfect gift; but I have not been content with what
I have. The desires of the flesh and the desires of the
eyes and pride in possessions have inflamed greed in my
heart. Like a Pharisee, I cleanse the outside of the cup
and dish, but inside I am full of greed and wickedness.
Have mercy upon me, O God, and forgive my sins of
greed:

My greed, which craves the worldly things that
cannot satisfy my soul;
My greed, which forgets your goodness and
faithfulness;
My greed, which seeks security in the mammon of
this world;

My greed, for personal power, popularity, and prestige;

My greed, which blinds me to the blessings you have lavished upon me;

My greed, which sours my spirit with ingratitude;

My greed, which stirs up strife with family or friends;

My greed, which deceives me into trusting in riches;

My greed, which conspires to deceive others for my gain;

My greed, which abuses power to pursue my selfish desires;

My greed, which cares more about my pleasures than my neighbor's need;

My greed, which kills the joy of generosity;

My greed, which prefers worldly wealth to heavenly treasure.

A PRAYER OF REPENTANCE AND TRANSFORMATION

O most gracious and generous God, have mercy upon me and forgive my sins of greed! You are the fountain of living water, but a greedy heart is a broken cistern that can hold no water. Deliver me from the power of mammon, that I might serve you with my whole heart! Grant me the grace to count all worldly things as worthless in comparison to the worth of knowing Christ Jesus my Lord! May the world be crucified to me, and I to the world, that I might live no longer for myself but for him who for my sake died and was raised. Sanctify my heart, that I may love you above all things, and love my neighbor as myself. Renew my mind and transform my life, that I may honor and serve you as a faithful steward of the resources you have entrusted to me. Change me from the inside out, so that, filled with joy and gratitude,

I will delight in doing good, be rich in good works, and be generous and ready to share, following Jesus who said, "It is more blessed to give than to receive." Amen.

THE ASSURANCE OF THE GOSPEL

For you know the grace of our Lord Jesus Christ, that though he was rich, yet for your sake he became poor, so that you by his poverty might become rich (2 Corinthians 8:9).

What then shall we say to these things? If God is for us, who can be against us? He who did not spare his own Son but gave him up for us all, how will he not also with him graciously give us all things? Who shall bring any charge against God's elect? It is God who justifies. Who is to condemn? Christ Jesus is the one who died— more than that, who was raised—who is at the right hand of God, who indeed is interceding for us (Romans 8:31-34).

Chapter 6

The Sin of Gluttony, and the Hungering Savior

Believers should not be satisfied with
general repentance. Rather, it is everyone's duty
to try to repent of every individual sin individually.

THE WESTMINSTER CONFESSION OF FAITH
in Modern English[1]

Then Jesus was led up by the Spirit into the wilderness to be tempted by the devil. And after fasting forty days and forty nights, he was hungry. And the tempter came and said to him, "If you are the Son of God, command these stones to become loaves of bread." But he answered, "It is written, 'Man shall not live by bread alone, but by every word that comes from the mouth of God.'"

Then the devil took him to the holy city and set him on the pinnacle of the temple and said to him, "If you are the Son of God, throw yourself down, for it is written, 'He will command his angels concerning you,' and 'On their hands they will bear you up, lest you strike your foot against a stone.'"

Jesus said to him, "Again it is written, 'You shall not put the Lord your God to the test.'"

Again, the devil took him to a very high mountain and showed him all the kingdoms of the world and their glory. And he said to him, "All these I will give you, if you will fall down and worship me." Then Jesus said to him, "Be gone, Satan! For it is written, 'You shall worship the Lord your God and him only shall you serve.'" Then the devil left him, and behold, angels came and were ministering to him (Matthew 4:1-11).

The repentance spoken of in the Westminster Confession and Catechisms (based on Scripture) is to be an ongoing repentance, as the Holy Spirit works continually in the life-long process of our sanctification to transform us more nearly into the likeness of Christ. This chapter addresses the sin – or sinful disposition – of **gluttony**. But before we *bite* into that one, I want to touch on some preliminary points.

We might think that only those who are overweight are guilty of gluttony. That's the first error that we need to reject. First of all, I know quite well from personal experience that a person can be gluttonous but still not be overweight. Looks can be deceiving. Of course, gluttony – especially when combined with physical sloth as it often is – may have its visible, physical consequences; but the much more important point is that gluttony is an invisible spiritual reality which resides within us all, no matter what our physical appearance.

Secondly, gluttony has to do not only with food but with all earthly things; hunger is a pang not only in the stomach but also in the soul. The question is: How do we seek to satisfy that hunger deep within us?

Gluttony, like greed, is a corrupted desire for God's good gifts in creation. In the beginning, God said,

> "Behold, I have given you every plant yielding seed that is on the face of the earth, and every tree with seed in its fruit. You shall have them for food" (Genesis 1:29).

Then after the flood in the days of Noah, God said,

> "Every moving thing that lives shall be food for you. And as I gave you the green plants, I give you everything" (Genesis 9:3).

Psalm 104 says that God provides "plants for man to cultivate," to "bring forth food from the earth, and wine to gladden the heart of man, oil to make his face shine and bread to strengthen man's heart" (Psalm 104:14-15). The Bible is filled with affirmations of the goodness of creation and the good gifts of God's providence for our earthly life. God wants us to enjoy good food! As Paul wrote to Timothy, God "richly provides us with everything to enjoy" (1 Timothy 6:17). The Scriptures also warn against false teachers who insist on strict dietary practices or other forms of asceticism (abstinence from certain foods). Paul wrote to Timothy,

> ...some will depart from the faith by devoting themselves to deceitful spirits and teachings of demons, through the insincerity of liars whose consciences are seared, who forbid marriage and require abstinence from foods that God created to be received with thanksgiving by those who believe and know the truth. For everything created by God is good, and nothing is to be rejected if it is received with thanks-

giving, for it is made holy by the word of God and prayer (1 Timothy 4:1-5).

To the Corinthians Paul wrote: "...whether you eat or drink, or whatever you do, do all to the glory of God" (1 Corinthians10:31).

The point: Food is a good gift from God. It glorifies God when with thanksgiving we eat the food he gives us so that we may serve him upon the earth. Food is a good gift from God; *but food is not God*. And that gets us right to the point. Like money, food becomes a god when it becomes the source and foundation of our happiness, our security, our joy, our *comfort*. That is the reason Jesus said, "Do not labor for the food that perishes, but for the food that endures to eternal life, which the Son of Man will give to you" (John 6:27).

Food cannot fill up that empty hole in your soul. Gluttony is the sin of looking to food to satisfy the craving of our souls for security, a sense of well-being, *comfort*, and *control* over our lives. But the happiness we seek from the things of this world is but bait on a barbed hook. And we bite it and bite it and bite it again – obsessively, compulsively, addictively – always hooked, but never satisfied. We seek to be filled by the things of this world, when only God himself can satisfy the hunger in our souls.

Jesus shows us what it means to hunger for God and to feed upon his word. The Scriptures record his forty-day fast in the wilderness, during which he prepared himself for his ministry for our salvation.

And after fasting forty days and forty nights, he was hungry. And the tempter came and said to him, "If you are the Son of God, command these stones to become bread." But he answered, "It is written, 'Man shall not live by bread alone, but by every word that comes from the mouth of God.'" (Matthew 4:2-4).

This was not a temptation to gluttony *per se*. But it gets to the gut of gluttony. It was a temptation for Jesus to abuse his power for the sake of meeting his immediate physical needs and desires. He could turn those stones into bread and eat; then he wouldn't be hungry anymore. And, after all, he was about to begin his great work of ministry; didn't he deserve to eat, shouldn't he eat?

But Jesus' answer shows us what was really at stake. It wasn't about stones and bread. It was about his faithfulness as God's Son, and about the fact that his strength for ministry would come not from physical bread but from the spiritual bread of the word of God. Jesus repelled the devil by quoting Scripture (Deuteronomy 8:3) – a Scripture which focuses on God as the true source of strength, the true sustenance of life. "Man shall not live by bread alone, but by every word that comes from the mouth of God" (Deuteronomy 8:3; Matthew 4:4).

Later in his ministry, Jesus would reiterate the same point with his disciples. The disciples were urging Jesus to eat – so he would keep up his strength for ministry – but Jesus said to them, "I have food to eat that you do not know about" (John 4:32). The disciples said, "Has anyone brought him something to eat?" And Jesus said to them, "My food is to do the will of him that sent me and to accomplish his work" (John 4:34).

Jesus' food was the word of God and the will of God. That reveals gluttony for what it really is. Gluttony is a hunger for earthly things as a substitute for God himself. Gluttony is a hunger for the "food" of this world which dulls and kills our hunger for God: our hunger for God's word, our hunger to do God's will, our hunger to glorify God's name. *And when we hunger for the good gifts of God more than for God himself, then we have become idolatrous gluttons.*

When we think of gluttony in this way, we can see that gluttony is not merely a matter of food, but any of the good earthly things that fill our lives. Do we have over-stuffed clothes closets? Is that any different from an over-stuffed stomach? But what happens when we walk by a shop window or browse the catalogs that clog our mailbox? It's gluttony! Do we have attics, basements, and storage rooms filled to overflowing with – you name it – *stuff* that gathers dust but will never be put to good use? Yet we can't find it in ourselves to get rid of it! Why do we cling to it? Why does it have such power over our lives that we let it clutter up our homes? Because we might *need* it some day. We just can't *bear* to part with it. Are these not little idols set up in their own special shrines in our homes? They clutter more than our attics and basements; they clutter our souls.

What about you? Do you have a gluttony for gadgets? A gluttony for entertainment? A gluttony for luxury and leisure? A gluttony for email, instant messaging and texting? All of these can become compulsively addictive, just as much as food. Do you have a gluttony for personal attention? Must you always be "center stage," the focus of every personal conversation – your activities, your needs, your accomplishments, your troubles? Some people are gluttons for sympathy; others are gluttons for praise and glory; either way, it's a gluttony for attention, which is self-idolatry.

When I go to a pastors' conference, and walk into the room set up as a theological bookstore, do I succumb to gluttony? *Far, far too often.* Do I have books that I have never read, and still buy more? Far, far too many! *"But it's a good book and I might read it one day!"* What is that? It is gluttony! When I walk into a sporting goods store, do I suddenly feel my need for all kinds of hunting equipment, that a moment before I had never even thought about? It's gluttony! It's gluttony because a shopping spree like that could just as easily be called a *"feeding frenzy."* It makes us feel good. Buying things is a way of getting our *"comfort food"* just as much as eating is. But it is always false comfort. And because it is false comfort, it is idolatry. And this kind of idolatry dulls our hunger for the living God. As John Piper has written, "...we are less sensitive to spiritual appetites when we are in the bondage of physical ones."[2]

And what happens when we fall into the bondage of physical appetites, consumed by our consumption? Unchecked, unrepented of, gluttony will ultimately destroy the soul with an all-pervasive selfishness. One of the best descriptions of the corrupting power of gluttony is found in the children's classic, ***Charlotte's Web***. Templeton the rat was a glutton. Even his "good deed" near the end of the story was done out of mere, sheer, self-interested, gluttonous selfishness. Here is the description of his character:

> The rat had no morals, no conscience, no scruples, no consideration, no decency, no milk of rodent kindness, no compunctions, no higher feeling, no friendliness, no anything. He would kill a gosling if he could get away with it – the goose knew that. Everybody knew it.[3]

Now, what does that describe? It reminds me of the proverbial warning the Apostle Paul wrote to Titus in Crete: "Cretans are always liars, evil beasts, lazy gluttons" (Titus 1:12). And in his letter to the Philippians, Paul warned of those who

> ...walk as enemies of the cross of Christ. Their end is destruction, their god is their belly, and they glory in their shame, with minds set on earthly things (Philippians 3:18-19).

Think about that phrase: "...their god is their belly ... with minds set on earthly things." That refers not simply to literal food in the literal belly; it is a figurative expression meaning that such people live only for themselves, as if this world is all there is, seeking always to satisfy their own selfish creature comforts, living and dying as beasts of the field: "evil beasts, lazy gluttons" (Titus 1:12).

And for the salvation of such corrupted souls, Jesus Christ, the Son of God, came into the world. Christ Jesus came into the world to save *gluttons!* How do I know that Jesus Christ came into the world to save gluttons? I'll tell you how I know: The Bible tells me so. The Bible tells me that Jesus Christ, the Creator Incarnate, by whom all things were made (John 1:3; Colossians 1:16), the Giver of every good and perfect gift, enjoyed dinner parties and wedding receptions. And he was often seen in the company of "tax-collectors and sinners," so much so that he was called "a friend of ...sinners"; indeed, Jesus himself was accused of being "a glutton and a drunkard!" (Matthew 11:19; Luke 7:34)

Oh, that was a false accusation; Jesus was not a glutton and a drunkard. But it was indeed true that he was "a friend of sinners." Yes, it's true; he befriended gluttons and drunkards. He befriended them to such a degree that he was "guilty by association"! And aren't you and I glad that he did? Aren't you and I glad that he still does?

What's really interesting about the false accusation that Jesus was "a glutton and a drunkard" is that *that* was an accusation which, if proven, could result in capital punishment according to Old Covenant Israelite law (Deuteronomy 21:20). The Pharisees who accused Jesus of being "a glutton and drunkard" were not merely slandering his character, not merely trying to ruin his reputation; they were accusing him of a capital offense, trying to establish grounds on which to *kill* him. Though there is no historical evidence that this law in Deuteronomy was ever prosecuted to the full extent (and it probably wasn't), there is no doubt that if it could have been prosecuted against Jesus it would have been. They would have killed him, just as surely as Templeton would have killed a gosling. And ultimately they did. They crucified the "friend of sinners" falsely accused of being "a glutton and a drunkard." *But it was for our gluttony that he died.*

See him there: the hungering Savior dying for gluttonous sinners. Jesus said, "My food is to do the will of him who sent me, and to accomplish his work" (John 4:34). Jesus hungered for God. Jesus hungered to do the will of God. **And Jesus' hunger to accomplish his Father's work led him to die for gluttons.**

Only Jesus Christ, the hungering Savior, can save you and me from our sins of gluttony, because in his hunger for our salvation, Jesus Christ identified himself with us in our gluttony – the friend of sinners! – even to the point that he was willing not only to be falsely accused of our gluttony but also to bear our sins of gluttony in his body on the tree and to suffer in our stead for our gluttony. There on the cross he ate the bitter herbs of God's judgment and drank the cup of the wine of God's wrath poured out upon him for our sake. He hungered to do the will of his Father; he hungered for our salvation; and so, on the cross, he *ate and drank* your death, and mine, under the wrath of God.

Meditate on this, and believe it: **Jesus hungered so that we, saved from our gluttony, might feast with him forever.** The prophet Isaiah proclaimed the gospel, saying,

> On this mountain the LORD of hosts will make
>   for all peoples
> a feast of rich food, a feast of well-aged wine,
>   of rich food full of marrow, of aged wine well
>   refined.
> And he will swallow up on this mountain
>   the covering that is cast over all peoples,
> the veil that is spread over all nations.
>   He will swallow up death forever;

and the Lord GOD will wipe away tears from all faces
…(Isaiah 25:6-8).

There is a feast of rich food prepared for all those who
trust in Jesus Christ. The day is coming when Christ shall
feast with his Bride, the church, those redeemed by his blood.
"Blessed are those who are invited to the marriage supper of
the Lamb!" (Revelation 19:9). The day will come when the
fast and famine of this world will be over, and the redeemed
of the Lord will feast for all eternity.

When the perishable puts on the imperishable, and
the mortal puts on immortality, then shall come to
pass the saying that is written:
    "Death is swallowed up in victory"
(1 Corinthians 15:54).

And that victory is your victory if you are *feeding* upon
Jesus Christ for your life.
    Jesus said, "I am the bread of life; whoever comes to me
shall not hunger, and whoever believes in me shall never
thirst" (John 6:35). ***Hunger for him who hungered for you,
and feast upon him forevermore!***

For Further Meditation and Spiritual Exercise

A CALL TO CONFESSION
    Be not among drunkards
or among gluttonous eaters of meat,
    for the drunkard and the glutton will come to
poverty, and slumber will clothe them with rags
(Proverbs 23:20).

The one who keeps the law is a son with understanding, but a companion of gluttons shames his father (Proverbs 28:7).

Let us walk properly as in the daytime, not in carousing and drunkenness, not in sexual immorality and sensuality, not in quarreling and jealousy. But put on the Lord Jesus Christ, and make no provision for the flesh, to gratify its desires (Romans 13:13).

A PRAYER OF CONFESSION

Almighty and eternal God, your goodness is seen throughout the works of creation, and you richly provide me with everything to enjoy. With faithfulness and power, you bring forth food from the earth, wine to gladden the heart of man, oil to make his face shine, and bread to strengthen man's heart. But I have abused your good gifts with my greed and gluttony, grasping more for myself, craving food that perishes rather than feasting on the food which endures to eternal life. Look upon me in mercy, and forgive my sins of gluttony:

My gluttony, which fills my stomach, while my heart is empty of gratitude;

My gluttony, which comforts my body physically but numbs my soul spiritually;

My gluttony, which craves for more and more things that satisfy less and less;

My gluttony, which obsesses on personal pleasure and luxury;

My gluttony, which rationalizes self-indulgence and ignores the needs of others;

My gluttony, which wastes money on unnecessary stuff;

My gluttony, which abuses my body which you have made for your glory;

My gluttony, which expresses my greed and leads to sloth;

My gluttony, which is my appetite for this world, when I should hunger for you.

A PRAYER OF REPENTANCE AND TRANSFORMATION

Have mercy upon me, O Lord, according to your steadfast love. According to your abundant mercy, blot out my transgressions of gluttony. O God, give me a heart that hungers for you! May your word be the food of my soul! May it be my meat and drink to do your will! May Jesus Christ be to me the true bread of life! May I receive all the gifts of your providence with thanksgiving, and may they be sanctified to me for the service of your Kingdom. May I receive every taste of food and drink and every bit of material blessing as a testimony of your goodness, faithfulness, generosity, and grace. Set me free from the slavery of gluttony, O God! Renew my mind, so that I will not be obsessed with the things of this world, and transform my life so that I may turn from self-indulgent gluttony to self-giving generosity. Change me from the inside out, that I may glorify you with my body. Grant me the grace of self-discipline and self-control by the power of the Holy Spirit, so that whether I eat or drink, or whatever I do, I may do all to your glory; through Jesus Christ our Lord. Amen.

THE ASSURANCE OF THE GOSPEL

Come, everyone who thirsts, come to the waters;
and he who has no money, come, buy and eat!
Come, buy wine and milk
without money and without price.

Why do you spend your money for that which is not
bread, and your labor for that which does not satisfy?
Listen diligently to me, and eat what is good,
and delight yourselves in rich food.
Incline your ear, and come to me;
hear, that your soul may live... (Isaiah 55:1-3).

Jesus said, "I am the bread of life; whoever comes to
me shall not hunger, and whoever believes in me shall
never thirst" (John 6:35).

If we say we have no sin, we deceive ourselves, and
the truth is not in us. If we confess our sins, he is faithful
and just to forgive us our sins and to cleanse us from all
unrighteousness (1 John 1:8-9).

Blessed are those who are invited to the marriage
supper of the Lamb (Revelation 19:9).

Chapter 7

The Sin of Lust,
and the Holy Savior

In this repentance, the sinner is able to see his
sins as God sees them, as filthy and hateful, and as
involving great danger to the sinner, because they are
completely contrary to the holy nature and righteous law
of God. Understanding that God in Christ is merciful to
those who repent, the sinner suffers deep sorrow for and
hates his sin, and so he determines to turn away from all
of them. And turning to God, he tries to walk with him
according to all his commandments.

THE WESTMINSTER CONFESSION OF FAITH
in Modern English[1]

Finally, then, brothers, we ask and urge you in the
Lord Jesus, that as you received from us how you
ought to live and to please God, just as you are doing,
that you do so more and more. For you know what
instructions we gave you through the Lord Jesus. For
this is the will of God, your sanctification: that you

abstain from sexual immorality; that each one of you know how to control his own body in holiness and honor, not in the passion of lust like the Gentiles who do not know God; that no one transgress and wrong his brother in this matter, because the Lord is an avenger in all these things, as we told you beforehand and solemnly warned you. For God has not called us for impurity, but in holiness. Therefore whoever disregards this, disregards not man but God, who gives his Holy Spirit to you (1 Thessalonians 4:1-8).

The last of the "seven deadly sins" is *lust*. Where's the best place for us to begin? The best place to begin is … "In the beginning."

In the beginning … …God said, "Let us make man in our image … ." So God created man in his own image … male and female he created them. …And God blessed them. And God said to them, "Be fruitful and multiply … ." (Genesis 1:1, 26-28).

Then, Genesis 2 gives us that beautiful picture of how God took one of the man's ribs and from it made a woman and brought her to the man. Then the man said, in the first lines of love poetry ever spoken:

"This at last is bone of my bones and flesh of my flesh … ." (Genesis 2:23).

Then the Scripture says:

Therefore a man shall leave his father and mother and hold fast to his wife, and they shall become one flesh. And the man and his wife were both naked and were not ashamed (Genesis 2:24-25).

That's where we must begin. In order for us to see lust for what it is, and why it is so offensive to God and dangerous for us, we must see clearly the Biblical vision of the beautiful and God-glorifying gift of human sexuality. In the beginning, God created humanity male and female; and the one-flesh sexual union of husband and wife is a beautiful and God-glorifying gift. We must begin right here, *in the beginning,* with the affirmation and celebration of marriage as an institution ordained of God, in the context of which the human race in general is to be propagated, and through which specifically the church is to be increased and spread throughout the earth by means of the one-flesh sexual union of husband and wife.[2]

And so, we begin here, *in the beginning*, with the affirmation and celebration of the God-ordained one-flesh sexual union of husband and wife as an expression of the unity of their heart and soul and spirit in perfect oneness, in ecstatic enjoyment of one another in the presence of God, to his glory!

You know, I can very easily imagine the world – the contemporary "cosmopolitan," liberated, sophisticated people – laughing and scoffing at, and mocking the sour-faced preacher in a black robe railing against the evils of lust. Can't you just imagine it? But you know what I would say to them? *Hey, I'm no priggish prude.* You see, as Christians, we don't believe that sex is dirty and naughty and shameful and bad. Quite to the contrary: The Bible reveals that God, the good Creator, implanted sexual desire within us, as part of our good humanity before sin ever entered the world. There is nothing sinful about sexual desire in and of itself; in fact, in and of itself, sexual desire is a good and healthy part of our human nature as created by God. True Christianity teaches that sex within marriage is good and beautiful and wonderful and brings glory to God. Sexual desire is not the problem. The problem is our sinful nature. The problem is sexual desire gone awry. The problem is something good being used for evil purposes. And that is the reason that lust (the temptation and desire for sexual fulfillment outside of marriage) is such an offense to God, because it is an ungrateful, unfaithful, selfish corruption and perversion and abuse of God's good gift.

This is an important principle which applies to all sin. *Sin is always an ungrateful, unfaithful, selfish corruption and perversion and abuse of God's good gift.* Sin is always a matter of taking one of God's blessings and ruining it. Sin is always a matter of turning something good into something bad.

And so, Satan tempts us with sexual lust in order to corrupt God's good gift. Satan tempts us with sexual lust in order to destroy that which is good, beautiful, and precious in God's sight. Satan tempts us with sexual lust in order to undermine and to destroy the institution of marriage. Satan tempts us with sexual lust in order to de-humanize men and women, reducing them to mere beasts of the field (causing us to forget, or to deny, that we are created in the image of God for his glory). Satan tempts us with sexual lust in order to hurt us and steal our joy, because Satan knows that sexual sin does great harm to us psychologically, emotionally, spiritually, and relationally.[3]

Lust is a lie. It is a lie designed to destroy your most precious relationships. It is a lie designed to ruin your life.

The first-century Greco-Roman world was a world filled with sexual immorality. Sexual immorality was one of the defining characteristics of first-century paganism, reaching even into the religious practices of Gentile idolatry. And so the Apostle Paul wrote to the Christians in Thessalonica who had formerly lived as pagans:

> Finally, then brothers, we ask and urge you in the Lord Jesus, that as you received from us how you

ought to walk and to please God, just as you are doing, that you do so more and more. For you know what instructions we gave you through the Lord Jesus. For this is the will of God, your sanctification: that you abstain from sexual immorality; that each one of you know how to control his own body in holiness and honor, not in the passion of lust like the Gentiles who do not know God ... (1 Thessalonians 4:1-5).

In this passage from First Thessalonians, the Scripture clearly states that sexual holiness is the revealed will of God for us and a specific necessity for our sanctification. "For this is the will of God, your sanctification: that you abstain from sexual immorality" (1 Thessalonians 4:3).

That word which is translated "sexual immorality" is a Greek word which would cover (or include) all sexual activity outside of marriage: premarital sex, adultery, homosexual practice, and any other sexual activity outside of marriage. The Greek word is *porneia*, from which we get the English word *pornography*. Pornography is, literally, *graphic sexual immorality*: sexual immorality graphically presented.

I hope we all know the dangers today, especially with Internet pornography providing such easy and private access to the temptations of lust. So, men, put a filter on your computer and let somebody else set the password. Now, does that sound like strict overkill? I don't think so. Somebody else I know, who has a lot more authority than I do, said, "If your right eye causes you to sin, tear it out and throw it away" (Matthew 5:29). Filters on computers sound like a pretty good option. What about when you travel alone on business? When you check in to the hotel at the front desk, you can tell them right there, before you ever go to your room: "Disconnect the pornography from the movie options." Then you don't have to worry about it. You give no opportunity to the devil.

Of course, there are many times in our culture when men can hardly avoid the obvious. In warm weather, it is not uncommon to see women running for exercise in their brightly-colored, eye-catching *underwear*! Well, men, you remember Driver's Ed: *Keep your eye on the road!* Otherwise, you might have a wreck ... and it might be a really, really bad wreck.

Let's face it; these days we have to be proactive in spiritual warfare. Give no opportunity to the devil. We have to set boundaries and keep them. No "working lunches" one-on-one with someone of the opposite gender. No "Happy Hour" socializing after work with "a friend" of the opposite gender. Traveling on business in mixed company from your office? Set your boundaries and find someone on that business trip who will hold you accountable. An exercise partner of the opposite gender? I don't think so. Do not be deceived:

> *For still our ancient foe*
> *doth seek to work us woe;*
> *his craft and power are great;*
> *and armed with cruel hate,*
> *on earth is not his equal.*[4]

Men, the word of God calls and commands us, saying:
> Drink water from your own cistern,
> flowing water from your own well. ...

> Let your fountain be blessed,
> and rejoice in the wife of your youth, a lovely deer,
> a graceful doe.

> Let her breasts fill you at all times with delight;
> be intoxicated always in her love.

> Why should you be intoxicated, my son, with a forbidden woman and embrace the bosom of an adulteress?

> For a man's ways are before the eyes of the LORD,
> and he ponders all his paths (Proverbs 5:15-21).

Proverbs 5 is filled with warnings against adultery, and the point is that it all begins in the *mind*, it all begins in the imagination. That is how Satan sows his seeds of deceit. So, men, we need to keep a watch on our eyes, our hearts, and our imaginations – and teach our sons to do the same. It's also important for us to be aware of the kind of triggers or stresses that can make us especially vulnerable to lust: things such as financial stress, work-related stress, anger or frustration in marriage, boredom with life in general, a little too much to drink, a little too much personal pride and power. Be aware of the triggers and stresses and situations that make you especially vulnerable, and set your boundaries and get the support and accountability you need.

Although most of the warnings in Scripture against lust are addressed specifically to men, probably due to the male psyche and the male sex drive, lust is not only a man's problem. Women have to deal with it also, though perhaps, generally speaking, from a different perspective. First of all, there is the basic issue of modesty and propriety in dress. To dress in such a way as to incite the lust of men is to participate in their sin of lust – even if that's *not* your intention. Christians ought to support one another and encourage one another by maintaining standards of modesty and propriety. It's a way of showing respect to one another and honoring marriage in the church and not being a stumbling-block to others (married or single). It is very important that we model appropriate dress for our young people. You can still dress very attractively and look very beautiful without dressing in a revealing and provocative way which incites lust. To incite lust with provocative dress or flirtation is to be guilty of lust.

I realize that quite often teenage girls don't really understand the importance of modest dress – or don't even really know how to judge what is appropriate and what is not. Parents, you need to teach them, with gentleness and patience and straightforward explanations. You need to be very clear with your teenage girls about the importance of modesty and propriety in dress, and tell them *why*.

A second way in which women are faced with the issue of lust is that in our contemporary culture, with the influence of radical feminism and other outgrowths of the so-called "sexual revolution," women are more and more being encouraged by the culture to be "just like men," that is, to become sexual predators actively on the hunt. You can read about it on the magazine covers at the checkout line in the grocery store. Although by God's design women's sexuality is much more a matter of emotional security (committed love) than mere physical pleasure, the culture is increasingly seeking to influence women to view sex primarily in terms of physical pleasure. This is not true liberation but is in fact a greater slavery to the chauvinistic worldview of sinful men. It plays right into the sinful desires of rogue men who have no intention of self-sacrificial love and commitment. And ultimately, it leaves women hurt, empty, and alone – no matter how many men they have hanging around.

And third, there is a kind of lust which I think is of particular danger to married women these days (it can also apply to men but I think it is especially dangerous for women). It is what I call "soul mate" lust. I don't mean to disparage the help that matching services can give to single people. What I am referring to, however, is the effect that those commercials can have on married couples, especially married women who feel that their emotional needs are not being met in their marriage. You could call it the lust for the perfectly compatible "soul mate." It's that special *someone* out there, *somewhere*, who has taken up residence in your imagination. It is **emotional lust**. And it is dangerous.

If in fact you feel that your emotional needs are not being met in marriage, there are much better ways of dealing with that than with setting your heart's imagination on another man whom you think is more loving and kind and romantic and empathetic. Even your imaginary "soul mate," if you ever found him, would be a fallen sinner! Just as men must set boundaries on physical lust and fight against it, so also women must set boundaries on emotional lust and fight against it. And men, that's also an admonition to us: We are to love our wives as Christ loved the church and gave himself up for her (Ephesians 5:25).

That brings us to the most important part of this chapter: **Jesus Christ, the Holy Savior, and his love for his Bride, the church.** In the beginning, when God created man and woman, and blessed their one-flesh union, he had in mind something more, something greater, something far more wonderful. God blessed the physical union of husband and wife because he intends it to be a living picture of the mystical union of Christ and the church (Ephesians 5:32). Marriage, including the one-flesh union, is to be a living illustration of Christ's self-giving, self-sacrificial love for the church, and of our complete and submissive trust in and respect for Christ our Lord. Therein is the sanctity of sexuality, to the glory of God. And in that marvelous passage in Ephesians 5, which speaks to us of the mystical union of Christ and the church, the promise of our salvation through our union with Christ, we hear the gospel of God's great love for us: "Christ loved the church and gave himself up for her" (Ephesians 5:25).

The church as the Bride of Christ is a corporate image of the church, including both men and women. Jesus Christ, the Holy Savior, had to die in order to unite himself with us, in order to wash us and cleanse us so that we might be holy and without blemish in union with him. The holy Savior – the completely faithful, ever true Son of God – came into the world to unite himself *not* with a Bride who was pure and perfect and sinless and spotless by her own virtue (that's not who we were, that's not who we are apart from Christ), but with a Bride who had already been stained with the sins of lust and immorality and idolatry, given over to the false lovers (the false gods) of this world.

If that is true of the church corporately (which it is), then it is certainly true of us as individuals. This is the good news: The holy Savior, the faithful One, the only One who has perfectly pure eyes and a perfectly pure heart and a perfectly pure body, is the One who can save you from all your sins of lust and immorality and sexual sin. **The blood of Jesus, the holy Savior, cleanses us from all sin.**

You know, don't you, that Jesus Christ, the holy Savior, had a reputation for befriending those whose souls had been ravaged by sexual sin? Do you know the story of the woman at the well of Samaria (John 4:7-26)? He changed her life, because he was the man that she had *really* been looking for all her life: She had been looking for the love of God, and she found it in him, the holy Savior, who would bear her sins in his body on the tree. Or, what about the woman who broke open that expensive alabaster jar and anointed Jesus? She was "a sinner," and we all know what that means. And she found true love in Jesus – divine love that forgives and sets free from the power of sin (Luke 7:36-50). His divine love that forgives and sets free came flowing forth in the blood of his cross. And then, of course, there was the woman caught in adultery (John 8:2-11). Jesus didn't condemn her – because he knew that he would be condemned in her place, so that she could go and live a new life, set free from the power of her sins. And for each one of these women, there were men who were just as guilty of sexual sin, all of whom needed the cleansing blood of the holy Savior, and the sanctifying power of the Holy Spirit.

So it is with us, men and women who are prone to look for love in all the wrong places; men and women with impure hearts and minds and bodies; men and women in desperate need to be washed clean and made holy. The holy Savior has come into the world to save sinners such as you and I. The holy Savior has come to set us free to live new lives free from the slavery of sin. The holy Savior has come to give life, life abundant, life eternal – to all those who otherwise would have died eternally from the deadly poison of idolatrous lust.

The church's one foundation is Jesus Christ, her Lord;
she is his new creation by water and the Word:
from heav'n he came and sought her to be his holy bride;
with his own blood he bought her, and for her life he died.[5]

For Further Meditation and Spiritual Exercise

A CALL TO CONFESSION

Jesus said, "From within, out of the heart of man, come evil thoughts, sexual immorality, theft, murder, adultery, coveting, wickedness, deceit, sensuality, envy, slander, pride, foolishness. All these evil things come from within, and they defile a person" (Mark 7:21-23).

Jesus said, "You have heard that it was said, 'You shall not commit adultery.' But I say to you that everyone who looks at a woman with lustful intent has already committed adultery with her in his heart. If your right eye causes you to sin, tear it out and throw it away. For it is better that you lose one of your members than that your whole body be thrown into hell" (Matthew 5:27-29).

For this is the will of God, your sanctification: that you abstain from sexual immorality; that each one of you know how to control his own body in holiness and honor, not in the passion of lust like the Gentiles who do not know God (1 Thessalonians 4:3-5).

A PRAYER OF CONFESSION

You, O Lord, created humanity, male and female, in your image; and you have declared the marriage bed good and holy. You ordained the holy union of husband and wife to reflect the mystery of the holy union of Christ and his Bride, the church. Yet I have abused and defiled your good gift with evil thoughts, words, and deeds. Forgive me, O Lord, my sins of lust:

My wandering eye of lust;
My wandering heart of lust;
My impure thoughts of lust;
My lust, which offends your holiness and dishonors marriage;
My lust, which seeks only the satisfaction of my desires;
My lust, which captures my attention and imagination;
My lust, which enjoys the alluring temptations of the world;
My lust, which I entertain and rationalize as acceptable;
My lust, which approves of the worldly fashions of immodesty;
My lust, which pushes the boundaries of propriety;
My lust, which wars against my sanctification;
My lust, which is idolatry;
My lust, which denies and contradicts the beauty of the gospel.

A PRAYER OF REPENTANCE AND TRANSFORMATION

Have mercy upon me, O God, according to your steadfast love; according to your abundant mercy, blot out my transgressions of lust. Wash me thoroughly from my iniquity, and cleanse me from my sin! For I know my transgressions, and my sin is ever before me. Hear my plea for mercy, and come to my rescue! Remember not, O God, and forgive, my sins of youthful passions. Do not now give me up to the lusts of my impure heart! Deliver me from the power of lust, the temptations of the flesh, and the lure of deceitful desires. May my mind dwell only on that which is honorable, pure, lovely, and worthy of praise. Give me the grace and power of the Holy Spirit, that I may flee all manner of sexual immorality and control my body in holiness and honor. May all my relationships uphold the sanctity of marriage. Give me a passion for your glory, a burning desire for the honor of your name, a holy love which longs for more intimate communion with you – to know the love of Christ which surpasses knowledge! Amen.

THE ASSURANCE OF THE GOSPEL

... he was wounded for our transgressions; he was crushed for our iniquities; upon him was the chastisement that brought us peace, and with his stripes we are healed.

All we like sheep have gone astray; we have turned every one to his own way; and the LORD has laid on him the iniquity of us all (Isaiah 53:5-6).

Therefore, if anyone is in Christ, he is a new creation. The old has passed away; behold, the new has come. All this is from God, who through Christ reconciled us to himself ... that is, in Christ God was reconciling the

119

world to himself, not counting their trespasses against them...(2 Corinthians 5:17-19).

For our sake he made him to be sin who knew no sin, so that in him we might become the righteousness of God (2 Corinthians 5:21).

...the blood of Jesus his Son cleanses us from all sin (1 John 1:7).

Jesus said, "Neither do I condemn you; go, and from now on sin no more" (John 8:11).

There is therefore now no condemnation for those who are in Christ Jesus (Romans 8:1).

How Are You Right with God?

In the preceding chapters, we have been looking at the painful reality of sin in our lives and the glorious realities of forgiveness and spiritual transformation freely offered through Jesus Christ: cleansing from the guilt of our sins, and freedom from the power of our sins. This is the essence of spiritual transformation through the love of God the Father, the grace of his Son, Jesus Christ, and the power of the Holy Spirit.

At the heart of the biblical gospel is the promise of salvation *by grace alone through faith alone in Christ alone.*

> For by grace you have been saved through faith. And this is not your own doing; it is the gift of God, not a result of works, so that no one may boast (Ephesians 2:8-9).

Even when we repent of our sins and seek to grow in godliness, we are still completely dependent upon the grace of God. We do not make ourselves right with God even by our best efforts. If a right relationship with God (our justification before him) depended on us and our "best efforts," we would have no hope. The good news (*the gospel!*), however, is that even when we are "at our worst" there is still hope! Our hope is not in ourselves but in Jesus Christ. He did for us what we could never do for ourselves. He lived a perfectly sinless, truly obedient life of righteousness before God: for us and our salvation. He, Jesus Christ, is the One and only One who has ever met the "good enough for God" standard. And he did that on our behalf.

As our sinless Savior, he offered himself up as the atoning sacrifice for all our sins. He claimed our sins as his own; as the Scripture says, "He himself bore our sins in his body on the tree ..." (1 Peter 2:24). He took our place under the judgment of God and by his death for us satisfied the justice of God against sin. When we, in repentance and faith, receive him as our Lord and Savior, we receive the forgiveness he has purchased for us by his death, freedom from the penalty due our sins; and, further, the righteousness of his sinless life is credited to us so that we have a right standing with God, and "there is therefore now no condemnation for those who are in Christ Jesus" (Romans 8:1).

This is the basis of the Christian life. Without this assurance of the gospel, the spiritual life has no foundation whatsoever. Without the work of Jesus Christ for us, all our works are in vain. But his work on the believer's behalf is never in vain. And so, as a word of instruction, assurance, and encouragement, and as a call to personal trust in Jesus Christ, the Heidelberg Catechism #60 asks:

How are you right with God?

Only by true faith in Jesus Christ.

Even though my conscience accuses me of having grievously sinned against all God's commandments and of never having kept any of them, and even though I am still inclined toward all evil, nevertheless, without my deserving it at all, out of sheer grace, God grants and credits to me the perfect satisfaction, righteousness, and holiness of Christ, as if I had never sinned nor been a sinner, as if I had been as perfectly obedient as Christ was obedient for me. All I need to do is to accept the gift of God with a believing heart.

(Romans 3:21-28; Galatians 2:16; Ephesians 2:8-9; Philippians 3:8-11; Romans 3:9-10; Romans 7:23; Titus 3:4-5; Romans 3:24; Ephesians 2:8; Romans 4:3-5 (Genesis 15:6); 2 Corinthians 5:17-19; 1 John 2:1-2; Romans 4:24-25; 2 Corinthians 5:21; John 3:18; Acts 16:30-31)

The words of the hymn, *Rock of Ages*, remind us all that our eternal salvation and spiritual transformation are found not in ourselves but in Jesus Christ. Whether you have been a faithful Christian from childhood, or have strayed far from the Lord and now desire to return to him, or if you are for the first time seeking a right relationship with God through faith in Jesus Christ, this hymn provides a prayer which you can offer from the depths of your heart.

Rock of Ages, cleft for me, let me hide myself in thee;
let the water and the blood, from thy riven side which flowed,
be of sin the double cure, cleanse me from its guilt and power.

Not the labors of my hands can fulfill thy law's demands;
could my zeal no respite know, could my tears forever flow,
all for sin could not atone; thou must save, and thou alone.

Nothing in my hand I bring, simply to thy cross I cling;
naked, come to thee for dress; helpless, look to thee for grace;
foul, I to the Fountain fly; wash me, Savior, or I die.

While I draw this fleeting breath, when mine eyelids close in death,
When I soar to worlds unknown, see thee on thy judgment throne,
Rock of Ages, cleft for me, let me hide myself in thee.[1]

ENDNOTES

Foreword

1. See Appendices 1 and 2.
2. **THE WESTMINSTER CONFESSION OF FAITH** in Modern English, ed. by Philip B. Rollinson (Livonia, Mich: Evangelical Presbyterian Church, 2004), ch. 15, par. 4.

Introduction: Spiritual Transformation

1. **THE SHORTER CATECHISM** in Modern English, ed. by Philip B. Rollinson (Livonia, Mich: Evangelical Presbyterian Church, 2004).
2. J. C. Ryle, *HOLINESS* (Durham: Evangelical Press, 1993), p. 1.
3. Cornelius Plantinga, Jr., *NOT THE WAY IT'S SUPPOSED TO BE: A Breviary of Sin* (Grand Rapids: Wm. B. Eerdmans, 1995), pp. ix-x.
4. **THE WESTMINSTER CONFESSION OF FAITH** in Modern English, ch.15, par. 5. "Believers should not be satisfied with general repentance. Rather, it is everyone's duty to try to repent of every individual sin individually" (Psalm 19:13; Luke 19:8; 1 Timothy 1:13, 15; Daniel 9; Nehemiah 9).

5. **THE SHORTER CATECHISM** in Modern English,
   #83: Are all sins equally evil? In the eyes of God some
   sins in themselves are more evil than others, and some
   are more evil because of the harm that results from them
   (Ezekiel 8:6, 13, 15; 1 John 5:16; Psalm 19:13; Psalm
   78:17, 32, 56). #84: What does every sin deserve? Every
   sin deserves God's anger and curse, both in this life
   and in the life to come (Ephesians 5:6; Galatians 3:10;
   Lamentations 3:39; Matthew 25:41).
6. **THE WESTMINSTER CONFESSION OF FAITH** in
   Modern English, ch.15, par. 4.

Chapter 1: Pride

1. Not all who are "rich and powerful in this world" believe
   that they have no need of God. This is not a blanket condemnation of the rich and powerful *per se;* the emphasis
   is on the phrase "who believe they have no need of
   God."
2. *When I Survey the Wondrous Cross*, Isaac Watts, 1709.

Chapter 2: Envy

1. That is, the exercise of our will.
2. *Breathe on Me, Breath of God,* Edwin Hatch, 1878.
   The word "breath" is a figurative synonym for the Holy
   Spirit. In both Hebrew and Greek, the word for *breath* is
   the same as the word for *spirit.*
3. The Latin word *sanctus,* from which we get the English
   word *sanctification,* means "holy."
4. This is not at all to suggest utter futility in the Christian
   life. The sanctifying Spirit of Christ enables his saints
   to grow in grace and to overcome the power of sin in
   various areas of our lives; but our sanctification is never
   completed or perfected in this life. "And so a continual

and irreconcilable war goes on in every believer" (**THE WESTMINSTER CONFESSION OF FAITH** in Modern English, ch. 13, par. 2).

5. Plantinga, p. 157.
6. 1 Peter 1:4
7. *Jesus! What a Friend for Sinners!*, J. Wilbur Chapman, 1910.

Chapter 3: Anger

1. **THE LARGER CATECHISM** in Modern English (Livonia: Evangelical Presbyterian Church, 2004).
2. **THE WESTMINSTER CONFESSION OF FAITH** in Modern English, ch. 15, par. 5.
3. John Owen, *OF THE MORTIFICATION OF SIN IN BELIEVERS*, commenting on Romans 8:13.
4. Written in 2009-2010.
5. John Calvin, *COMMENTARY ON THE EPISTLE TO THE EPHESIANS* (Grand Rapids: Baker Book House, 1991), Vol. XXI, p. 298, on Ephesians 4:26.
6. Ibid.
7. Attributed to Ambrose Bierce.
8. Calvin, p. 298.
9. I am not referring to cases of justifiable physical self-defense or the physical defense of another person; nor am I denying that there are cases in which some form of restitution is appropriate and ought to be required as a matter of justice (but not vengeance). Also, the civil magistrate, as a servant of God, "bears the sword" against the wrongdoer in legal criminal and civil cases (Romans 13:1-4).

Chapter 4: Sloth

1. **THE HEIDELBERG CATECHISM** *with Scripture Texts* (Grand Rapids: CRC Publications, 1989).
2. Written in 2009-10, during which unemployment in the USA reached 10%.

Chapter 5: Greed

1. **THE WESTMINSTER CONFESSION OF FAITH** in Modern English, ch. 15, par. 4.
2. Written in 2009-10.
3. You may compare various English translations of Matthew 23:25, Luke 11:39, and Philippians 2:6.
4. "Will man rob God? Yet you are robbing me. But you say, 'How have we robbed you?' In your tithes and contributions" (Malachi 3:8).

Chapter 6: Gluttony

1. **THE WESTMINSTER CONFESSION OF FAITH** in Modern English, ch. 15, par. 5.
2. John Piper, *A HUNGER FOR GOD* (Wheaton, IL: Crossway Books, 1997), p. 90. I would highly commend this as the best book I have ever read concerning fasting.
3. E. B. White, *CHARLOTTE'S WEB* (New York: HarperTrophy, 1952, 1980), p. 46.

Chapter 7: Lust

1. **THE WESTMINSTER CONFESSION OF FAITH** in Modern English, ch. 15, par. 2.
2. "Did he not make them one, with a portion of the Spirit in their union? And what was the one God seeking?

Godly offspring. So guard yourselves in your spirit, and let none of you be faithless to the wife of your youth" (Malachi 2:15).

3. And, of course, sexual sin can also result in great physical harm as well.

4. *A Mighty Fortress is Our God,* Martin Luther, 1529; trans. by F.H. Hedge, 1853.

5. *The Church's One Foundation*, Samuel J. Stone, 1866.

Afterword: How Are You Right with God?

1. *Rock of Ages, Cleft for Me*, Augustus M. Toplady, 1776.

Appendix 1

Concerning the Westminster Confession of Faith and Catechisms

The Westminster Standards include the **Confession of Faith,** the **Larger Catechism** and the **Shorter Catechism.** By order of the English Parliament these documents were drafted (during the English Civil War) by the Westminster Assembly which met first on July 1, 1643, consisting of 151 persons appointed by Parliament. The members conducted 1,163 meetings, concluding their work on February 22, 1649.

Since their original publication, the Westminster Confession and Catechisms have served as the basis of the confessional documents of many Presbyterian and Reformed churches throughout the world. The standards came to New England with the Puritans and to the Middle Atlantic states with the Scotch-Irish Presbyterians. In 1729, the standards were adopted as the confessional position of a newly organized Presbyterian synod in the colonies and have played a substantial role in American Presbyterianism to the present day.

The version of the Westminster Standards used in this book is the modern English edition (The Summertown Company, Inc., 1974) which was adopted by the Evangelical Presbyterian Church in 1984 as the confessional standard of that denomination, of which the author of this book is a member. The Scriptural proof texts cited to support the Confession and Catechisms are a composite of all those cited in the various versions of the standards (British and American).

The Westminster Standards, although a majestic and systematic presentation of the truth of Holy Scripture, are of course human documents. They claim no divine authority, inspiration, inerrancy, or infallibility of their own; nor do those in the Reformed and Presbyterian tradition who hold to them attribute any ultimate and final authority to them. The Westminster Confession of Faith opens in chapter 1 with one of the most impressive affirmations of the divine inspiration and authority of Scripture ever penned. In paragraph 4, it states:

> The Bible speaks authoritatively and so deserves to be believed and obeyed. This authority does not depend on the testimony of any man or church but completely on God, its author, who is himself truth. The Bible therefore is to be accepted as true, because it is the word of God.
> (2 Peter 1:19, 21; 2 Timothy 3:16; 1 John 5:9; 1 Thessalonians 2:13; Galatians 1:11-12).

Appendix 2

Concerning the Heidelberg Catechism

In 1562, Frederick III, who ruled the German province of the Palatinate, commissioned the preparation of a new catechism to guide ministers and teachers in instructing the people in the Christian faith. Tradition credits two young men of Heidelberg – Zacharias Ursinus, a theology professor, and Caspar Olevianus, a preacher in the city – as the primary authors.

The catechism was approved by a synod in Heidelberg and published in January of 1563. Since its original publication, it has been translated into many European, Asian, and African languages. In 1968 the Synod of the Christian Reformed Church (CRC) appointed a committee to prepare "a modern and accurate translation" in English. The new English translation was approved in 1975, and some editorial revisions were adopted in 1988. Quotations of the Heidelberg Catechism in this book are from this version, published in 1989 by CRC Publications.

The overarching structure of the Heidelberg Catechism is formed by three major divisions which correspond to the basic outline of the Christian faith and life: our guilt (sin),

God's grace through Jesus Christ (salvation), and the believer's joyful response of gratitude (service). Within these three major divisions, the catechism is subdivided into fifty-two sections, so that a minister may use the catechism as a guide to preaching on each Lord's Day of the year. As a basic primer of Christian doctrine, the Heidelberg Catechism teaches the essential points of The Apostles' Creed, The Ten Commandments, and The Lord's Prayer. Scriptural texts provide the basis for all that is taught in this catechism.

The Heidelberg Catechism is particularly appealing due to its warm and personal tone. The questions are personally addressed to "you," and the answers are given in the first person so that the student responds with a personal expression of faith and not mere intellectual knowledge. The answer to the first question not only illustrates the personal tone of the catechism but also provides a concise summary of the whole catechism itself as it outlines the Christian faith and life in terms of guilt (sin), grace (salvation), and gratitude (service).

What is your only comfort in life and in death?

That I am not my own, but belong – body and soul, in life and in death – to my faithful Savior Jesus Christ.

He has fully paid for all my sins with his precious blood, and has set me free from the tyranny of the devil. He also watches over me in such a way that not a hair can fall from my head without the will of my Father in heaven: in fact, all things must work together for my salvation.

Because I belong to him, Christ, by his Holy Spirit, assures me of eternal life and makes me wholeheartedly willing and ready from now on to live for him.

(1 Corinthians 6:19-20; Romans 14:7-9; 1 Corinthians 3:23; Titus 2:14; 1 Peter 1:18-19; 1 John 1:7-9; 1 John 2:2; John 8:34-36; Hebrews 2:14-15; 1 John 3:1-11; John 6:39-40; John 10:27-30; 2 Thessalonians 3:3; 1 Peter 1:5; Matthew 10:29-31; Luke 21:16-18; Romans 8:28; Romans 8:15-16; 2 Corinthians 1:21-22; 2 Corinthians 5:5; Ephesians 1:13-14; Romans 8:1-17)

Bibliography

Calvin, John. *COMMENTARY ON THE EPISTLE TO THE EPHESIANS*, trans. by Wm. Pringle (Grand Rapids: Baker Book House, 1981).

Piper, John. *A HUNGER FOR GOD* (Wheaton, IL: Crossway Books, 1997).

Plantinga, Cornelius. *NOT THE WAY IT'S SUPPOSED TO BE: A Breviary of Sin* (Grand Rapids: Wm. B. Eerdmans, 1995)

Ryle, J. C. *HOLINESS* (Durham: Evangelical Press, 1993).

TRINITY HYMNAL (Norcross, GA: Great Commission Publications, Inc., 1990).

White, E. B. *CHARLOTTE'S WEB* (New York: HarperTrophy, 1952, 1980).

Theological Resources

NEW INTERNATIONAL VERSION *SPIRIT OF THE REFORMATION STUDY BIBLE* (Grand Rapids: Zondervan, 2003).

THE ESV STUDY BIBLE, English Standard Version, (Wheaton, IL: Crossway Bibles, 2008).

THE HEIDELBERG CATECHISM *with Scripture Texts* (Grand Rapids: CRC Publications, 1989).

THE WESTMINSTER CONFESSION OF FAITH and CATECHISMS in Modern English, ed. by Philip B. Rollinson (Livonia, Mich: Evangelical Presbyterian Church, 2004).

For more information on the Westminster Confession of Faith and Catechisms and the Heidelberg Catechism, please see the appendices.